Sixty-One Worship Talks for Children

Sixty-One
WORSHIP TALKS
for Children

with suggested objects for illustration

BY ELDON WEISHEIT

CONCORDIA
PUBLISHING HOUSE

Concordia Publishing House, St. Louis, Missouri
© 1968 Concordia Publishing House

Library of Congress Catalog Card No. 68-20728

5 6 7 8 9 10 11 12 13 CB 89 88 87 86 85 84 83

MANUFACTURED IN THE UNITED STATES OF AMERICA

To my three sons

Dirk
Tim
Wes

Contents

Preface

People remember what they see. Jesus stood by a stack of fish when He told four of His followers that they would be fishers of men. The analogy still survives. He gave new meaning to everyday items such as a mustard seed, the lilies of the field, a fruitless fig tree, a marriage supper. By His parables He not only made His message more easily understood, but He also gave His hearers constant reminders of that message as they continued to see the everyday objects and events that were used to illustrate His teachings.

The value of the object lessons in the children's sermons in this book is not based on their ability to attract attention or to satisfy the itching eye of today's TV-oriented society. They are to illustrate, to explain the simple truths of God's redeeming action in Christ. But they are also to tie visual strings around the fingers of the hearers so the lesson may be recalled as the object is encountered in daily life. For this reason the objects are not just something to look at but something to see in action. Objects are used not as something on a display shelf but as things used in the normal activity of the hearers.

These sermons were prepared for, and the majority used in, the regular Sunday morning worship service, and they readily became a part of the worship life of the congregation. As a part of a liturgical service they were used between the

Creed and the sermon hymn and were delivered from the lectern. However, many of them have also been used for worship services in the Christian day school and for Sunday school openings. Some have been adapted to TV devotions.

My thanks to the members of Trinity Lutheran Church, McComb, and Immanuel Lutheran Church, Hazlehurst, Miss., my first parish, and to my present congregation, The Lutheran Church of the Epiphany, Montgomery, Ala. Without the encouragement of these people this book would have remained a few outlines in the file drawer. Also my appreciation to my wife, Carolyn, who not only typed the final copy but claimed that she enjoyed it. Finally my public expression of thanks to the Holy Spirit who proclaimed to me the love of Christ in the texts I have used in the hope of passing the same message on to others.

ELDON WEISHEIT

Montgomery, Ala.

Sixty-One Worship Talks for Children

What Is the Alarm?

The Word

Besides this you know what hour it is, how it is full time now for you to wake from sleep. For salvation is nearer to us now than when we first believed. Romans 13:11 (From the Epistle for the First Sunday in Advent)

The World

An alarm clock and a toy fire truck

Did you hear the alarm in our Bible reading? It tells us to wake up. It warns us to watch the time because something important is about to happen. To understand the alarm, let's think about two kinds of alarms.

This fire truck in my hand reminds you of one kind of an alarm. When you hear a fire alarm, you know that the fire has already started. The sound of the siren on a fire truck doesn't tell you to prevent fires. It says to put the fire out.

This clock [*show clock*] is another kind of alarm. When this alarm goes off, it does not mean that anything has already happened. Instead it tells you that something is going to happen; so you had better get ready. When the alarm goes off you know that school will start soon. It is time to get ready.

There are also two kinds of alarms that tell us about Judgment Day, the final day of this earth. One alarm will be the sound of the angel's trumpet on the last day. That alarm is like the fire alarm. It means that the event has already started. When the trumpet sounds, it will be too late to get ready for Judgment Day.

But there is another kind of alarm for Judgment Day. It tells us that the Day is coming. It doesn't say when, but we know that it is nearer than ever before. It tells us to be prepared at all times. Our text is this kind of alarm when it says, "It is full time now for you to wake from sleep. For salvation is nearer to us now than when we first believed."

We appreciate this kind of alarm because it gives us a chance to think about Judgment Day before it happens. If Christ were a stranger, this alarm which tells us that He is coming might frighten us. But He is not a stranger. You already know how He first came to earth as the baby in Bethlehem. You know how He loved all people. You know how He died for your sins and arose from the dead to fulfill His promise that you could live forever with Him.

Since you do know these things about Christ, the text which tells you that He is coming again does not frighten you. Instead, it tells you to believe in Him. Believe that the Christ who is coming is the same Christ who has already come to be your Savior. Believe that He will come with the same love. Believe that He will come to fulfill His promises.

During Advent we often talk about Christ's coming. Each time you hear of His coming, let it sound like the excitement of an alarm clock when it wakes you up for a wonderful trip. Amen.

A Letter for Me?

For whatever was written in former days was written for our instruction, that by steadfastness and by the encouragement of the Scriptures we might have hope. Romans 15:4 (From the Epistle for the Second Sunday in Advent)

The World

A sealed envelope and a Bible

Probably most of the mail that comes to your house is for your mother or your father. But once in a while there may be a letter for you. Here is one right now. If this letter were for you, what would you do with it? Would you keep it till tomorrow or next week? Would you put the envelope in a frame and hang it on the wall? Of course not. Mail is to be read. You would open your letter and read it. You read all the mail you receive. Or do you?

The Bible is a letter from God to you and others. Many people leave their Bibles unopened. Others read the Bible as though they are reading someone else's mail. They don't apply it to their own lives. But how about you? Do you know that the Bible is God's letter to you?

You can be sure that the Bible is God's letter to you even though it is not addressed to your name and street number. Instead of listing the names of all the people for whom the Bible is intended, it describes the people. The Bible is sent to sinners, to those who have disobeyed God's law. That means

15

that it is sent to you and to me. But the Bible tells us more than just that we are sinners. In our Bible reading Paul says that it was written so that we might have encouragement and hope.

Because the Bible offers you this message of encouragement and hope, you can know that it is addressed to you. Christ died for all people. His death and resurrection gives us hope because in Him our sins have been removed and we are reunited with God. When the Bible says that Christ died for the sins of the whole world, it assures you that the message is addressed to you.

Since the Bible is God's letter to you, you should read it as though God were speaking to you. The Law will say, "John, honor your father and mother." "Susie, do not bear false witness." Also read the Gospel as it applies to you: "God so loved Tim that He gave His only-begotten Son that Tim might believe in Him and not perish but have everlasting life." "By grace Sharon is saved through faith, it is a gift of God, not of works."

When you read the Bible that way, you won't forget to keep on reading your mail from God. The Bible is God's letter of good news to you every day. Amen.

Your Job for God

The Word

This is how one should regard us, as servants of Christ and stewards of the mysteries of God. 1 Cor. 4:1 (From the Epistle for the Third Sunday in Advent)

The World

Christmas seals and a small stack of envelopes

These days before Christmas are a busy time. Suppose your mother asked you to help with the Christmas cards. Your job is to put the Christmas seals on the envelopes. Your mother tells you exactly how she wants it done. One seal on each envelope, placed right here [*on the back, middle of the flap*].

So you start to work. Soon your sister comes along to watch what you are doing. "Why are you putting the seals on the back where no one can see them?" she asks. She is right. No one will see them there. So you go back through all the envelopes and add another seal — right here [*front side, upper left-hand corner*].

Then one of your friends comes in to see if you can play. But you are busy; so he watches. "Say," he says, "I think these seals look better if you put two together." After thinking about it, you agree with your friend. So from then on you put two seals here [*lower left-hand corner of the front.*]

About that time your mother comes to check on how you are doing. You tell her that you have used all the seals but have many more envelopes. She tells you that there were the

17

same number of stamps as envelopes. Then she sees what you have done. "You did it wrong," she says; "I wanted to put the return address in this corner, and you have a stamp there. And you put too many stamps on each envelope. Now we don't have enough."

When you explain about the sister's and friend's suggestions, she asks you, "Whom were you helping? Me? Or someone else?"

Paul asks us the same question in our Bible reading. He says that we are to account of ourselves as ministers of Christ. We serve Christ and are responsible to Him. Christ has taken our place in punishment by dying for us. Now we are to live for Him. We are all His ministers; that is, we serve Him.

But often we would rather do things our own way. When we think that we can do things our own way because it is our life, we forget that Christ has paid for our lives so that we can live. Our job is to serve Him, not ourselves.

Sometimes we let other people tell us how we should serve God. They find fault with what we do and offer suggestions. When this happens we should remember whom we serve. We don't have to please all people. That is impossible. But we serve Christ. He loves us. We want to do what we can to love Him. Then we are faithful ministers of Christ. Amen.

Help Is as Near as . . .

The Word

Rejoice in the Lord always; again I will say, Rejoice. Let all men know your forbearance. The Lord is at hand. Philippians 4:4-5 (From the Epistle for the Fourth Sunday in Advent)

The World

A toy telephone, or a telephone that can be released from the jack

You have heard the advertisement, "Help is as near as your telephone." That is a comforting thought; especially when you are alone. There are many times when you need help. It is comforting to telephone and call someone for help.

But the statement "Help is as near as your telephone" isn't quite true. Suppose, for example, your house is on fire. You reach for the telephone. But the phone won't put out the fire. It will allow you to talk to the fire station and to ask that a truck be sent. But the help will have to come from the fire station. It may take them several minutes to get to your house. You can use the telephone to call doctors, police, or anyone you need. But it still takes time for the help to come to you.

In some ways prayer is like a telephone. With a telephone you can call someone for help. With prayer you can ask God for help. But the big difference is that when you call God for help you don't have to wait for Him to arrive. God is not waiting up in heaven for you to ask Him for help before He

19

starts the trip down to your house. God is here. Help is as near as God is, and He is with us at all times.

We know that God is with us, because Christ came to earth to be our Savior. As we wait for Christmas, we are not waiting for Him to be born again. At Christmas we celebrate the anniversary of His birth. The anniversary is important not just because He was born over 1900 years ago but because He is still with us today.

Sometimes people forget that God is with us. That is why Paul wrote to the people in Philippi and told them, "The Lord is at hand." He told the people to be happy about it. We also observe Christmas to remind ourselves that God is with us. So we rejoice again and again.

As we rejoice because God is with us in Christ, our lives are changed. Paul tells us that others will see our forbearance; which means our kindness, our gentleness, the understanding we have for others. Our rejoicing about God being with us is expressed not only in songs and Christmas greetings but also in the way we live. Because God is with us, we don't have to live in fear. Because He is with us, we don't have to be selfish; we don't have to live just for our own needs. Because God is with us, we have His help at all times. Let's use it. Let's rejoice about it. Amen.

What Did You Get Last Christmas?

The Word

[Christ] gave Himself for us to redeem us from all iniquity and to purify for Himself a people of His own who are zealous for good deeds. Titus 2:14 (From the Epistle for Christmas Day)

The World

Billfold, necktie, and money clip (or variations of these gifts from past Christmases)

The big question today is, "What did you get for Christmas?" I want to ask you a different question, "What did you get last Christmas?" It is not an unfair question. I can tell how much you appreciate your past gifts by how you remember them and how you used them. Then we'll know how much you appreciate the gifts you receive today. To show you how this works, I'll tell you about some of my past gifts.

I received this money clip one time. It's a nice clip, but I'm not in the habit of carrying a money clip; so I've never used it. Of course, I keep it in a box in my drawer. This necktie was also a gift. I like it. You've seen me wear it. Of course, I don't wear it every day. But I wear it at least two or three times a month. This billfold was also a gift. Even though I have other billfolds, I always use this one. I can't drive without it because my driver's license is in it. I can't buy anything without it because it carries my money and credit cards. In fact, you can tell who I am from this gift because it carries all my identification.

Now about your gift last Christmas. You received Christ, just as you do today and every day. But what kind of a gift was He? Was He a gift like my money clip — very nice but not so usable? Was He like my necktie — you use Him two or three times a month? Or was He like the billfold? Is He needed in your daily life? Is He so important that you couldn't get along without Him? Do you receive your identification from Him?

The Bible text tells us how to use the gift of Christ. Listen: "(Christ) gave Himself for us to redeem us from all iniquity and to purify for Himself a people of His own who are zealous for good deeds." Christ gives you the gift of forgiveness of sins.

You use this gift each time you confess your sins to Christ by telling Him how you need His help. You use this gift when you share the forgiveness He gives you by forgiving others. You use it when you remember that you can love others because Christ loves you.

Do you use the gift that you have? I'll ask you again next Christmas. Amen.

Do Not Open Before Christmas

The Word

But when the time had fully come, God sent forth His Son, born of woman, born under the Law, to redeem those who were under the Law, so that we might receive adoption as sons. Galatians 4:4-5 (From the Epistle for the First Sunday After Christmas)

The World

A package wrapped in Christmas paper and with a label: "Do not open before Christmas"

This package looks out of place today. All the other gifts have been opened and the paper thrown away. But this package is a problem. It has a label which says, "Do not open before Christmas." If the gift had arrived two weeks ago, there would have been no problem. We would have had to wait until December 25th. But this package is here today. Next Christmas is almost a year away. Do you think we should keep this gift until next Christmas? Would you if it were addressed to you? Of course not. The label says, "Do not open before Christmas." But it is not before Christmas anymore. It is after Christmas. We can open the package now.

But there is a more important gift than this package. It is the gift which we received several days ago, the gift of Jesus Christ. It is the greatest gift ever given. In Christ, God came into human flesh. He became like us so He could die for us and pay for our sins. At Christmas God gave Himself to us.

However, we need God with us every day — not just on

Christmas Day. We need His presence today, tomorrow, and all of next year. Sometimes people feel that Christmas is a joy reserved for December 25th. Now they have to wait for almost a year before they can have that joy again. But that is not true anymore. In the Old Testament the people waited for the gift. They had been promised a Savior, but they had not yet received the gift. It was as though the promise had a sign on it, "Do not open until Christmas."

But Christmas did come. Paul describes it as the fullness of time — that time when Christ did become human flesh for us. From then on we have lived after Christmas. Never again do we have to wait for the promise to be fulfilled. It is fulfilled for now and for all time. Christ came as a man in human flesh. He is our Savior. We still live in the fullness of time because the Holy Spirit still brings us the message of Christ in our lives. All that He did applies also to us. He gives us a gift every day because He gave us Himself. Amen.

The Tie That Binds

The Word

There is neither Jew nor Greek, there is neither slave nor free, there is neither male nor female; for you are all one in Christ Jesus. Galatians 3:28 (From the Epistle for New Year's Day)

The World

A calendar of the new year with the pages separated for easy showing

Happy New Year to you! And here is your new year — at least a symbol of the year that begins today. As you look at the 12 months ahead, you know that many things will happen. The 12 months are all part of the same year; yet each month will be different. Some months will be school months and others will be vacation months. Some will be hot and some will be cold. Some months will be filled with excitement and happiness. Others will seem dull and uneventful. Yet all the months are bound together into one year.

In the same way the church is made up of many kinds of people. Paul says it this way: "There is neither Jew nor Greek, there is neither slave nor free, there is neither male nor female; for you are all one in Christ Jesus." That is a good description of the church. The church is not a club for poor people or for rich people, for black people or white people, for men or women. The church is for sinners who believe in Jesus Christ as their Savior. The one thing that ties these 12 months together is not that they are exactly alike, but that they all belong to the same year. The one thing that binds

Christians together is not that they agree on everything, not that they happen to like one another or happen to be like one another. Christians are bound together by the one Christ who died for them all.

If you decided that you liked only the summer months, you might try to make your own year. You could take June, July, and August from this year, reach back to last year's calendar for the same months, and look ahead to next year for the summer months. If you put all of these together, you might have a calendar, but it would not be a year. It would just be a collection of your own making.

So also we cannot decide whom we want in our church. The tie that binds us together in our church cannot be our money, our education, our political views, or anything else except the grace of God given to us through Christ. If other things bind us together, then we are a club of our own making rather than a church united by Christ. But we do have Christ. He is the tie that binds us together not just today and not just for this year, but forever. The church is important to us because all in it share the love of Christ. In sharing this love of Christ, we give others forgiveness and understanding. And they give the same to us. Amen.

The Right Way to Stand Out

The Word

If you are reproached for the name of Christ, you are blessed, because the spirit of glory and of God rests upon you. But let none of you suffer as a murderer, or a thief, or a wrongdoer, or a mischief-maker. 1 Peter 4:14-15 (From the Epistle for the Sunday After New Year)

The World

A fourth-grade child

Kathy, would you please come to the front. Do you know why I asked you to come up here, Kathy? One reason is that I wanted everyone here to think about you. They are thinking about you now. That is nice for you. All of us like to have others think about us. But much could depend on what they are thinking. There could be two different reasons for calling someone to the front so that everyone else may think about that person.

The first reason is a bad one. What if I called Kathy in front to say that she was causing trouble in Sunday school? If I said that she disturbed others, that she didn't do her home work, that she was always late; Kathy would be embarrassed. She would rather not have others think about her. Of course, those things are not true about Kathy.

The other reason why I could call her to the front is a good one. I might want to say that Kathy is an outstanding Sunday school student. She has perfect attendance, she knows her lesson, she behaves well. If I said those things, Kathy would be glad to be in front. She would be a good example rather than a bad one.

In either case Kathy would stand out in the crowd, either in a good way or in a bad way. In the same way you may sometimes stand out in a crowd when others find fault with you, laugh at you, or tease you. If this happens to you, remember that there are two reasons why these things might happen.

One reason is that you may have done wrong. Then you are suffering for your own wrong. St. Peter tells us that we should not do wrong things. If we do, we are suffering justly.

There is another reason why you may be laughed at or criticized. It may be because you did what was right. St. Peter also tells us that others will find fault with us when we follow Christ. Maybe someone will laugh at you for going to Sunday school. Others may tease you because you won't go along with a crowd that is doing wrong. It makes us unhappy to have others laugh at us. Sometimes people do bad things just to avoid the ridicule of others.

Peter asks you to be happy when others criticize you for the sake of Christ. It is a good way to stand out. The world found fault with Christ too. They will find fault when they see Christ in you. But when you follow Christ because He is your Savior, when you love Him because He loves you, then you can take the criticism with joy. It is a joy that you have because you are with Christ. Amen.

Light from Both Sides

The Word

For behold, darkness shall cover the earth, and thick darkness the peoples; but the Lord will arise upon you, and His glory will be seen upon you. And nations shall come to your light, and kings to the brightness of your rising. Isaiah 60:2-3 (From the Epistle for Epiphany)

The World

A flashlight and a vanity mirror

Pretend that this flashlight is Christ. He is called the Light of the world; so, of course, this light can be only a symbol of His light. Think what it means when the light of Christ shines on you. It is a beacon that calls you to God. The Light shows you the way of life now and forever. You were in the darkness of sin, but the Light changes darkness to day. The Light chases away fears and gives us the comfort of God's presence. We have all of this because Christ has brought His light into our lives.

But many people refuse to look at this Light of the world. They turn their backs on the Light. [*Hold light behind head. Bring light to front but turn at the same time to keep light behind head.*] Isaiah speaks of people living in darkness. They are the ones who have turned from the Light. It is sad for us to be in the Light and to know that others are still in darkness.

But there is something you can do. You can be like this mirror. The mirror has no light, but it will reflect light. See!

29

[*Hold mirror facing people and light facing the mirror.*]
Even though the light was pointed in the other direction, you
could see the light in the mirror. When people turn their back
on the light [*hold light behind head*] they can still see you.
In you they can see light. It is not your light but a reflection
of the Light of the world. It is the same Light that called you
to God. When others see the love of Christ in you, it also
calls them to God. When you follow the Light of Christ as
He shows you the way of life now and forever, He will also
be leading others through you. Remember the mirror cannot
reflect light unless there is a light shining on it. So also you
can't reflect Christ unless you see Him and believe Him.

Arise and shine. Hear about Christ. Believe in Him. Let
Christ be seen in your life. Amen.

What Is Your Model?

The Word

Do not be conformed to this world but be transformed by the renewal of your mind, that you may prove what is the will of God, what is good and acceptable and perfect. Romans 12:2 (From the Epistle for the First Sunday After Epiphany)

The World

A ball of modeling clay, a golf ball, a building block, and a cross

Paul told you in the reading from Romans not to be conformed to this world, but to be transformed to the will of God. That means that you are not supposed to become like the world. Instead you are supposed to become like God. That sounds impossible. But let's think about it.

In one way you and I are like a ball of modeling clay. You've played with clay enough to know that it can be shaped any way you want. Modeling clay never shapes itself. By itself it is just a glob. But it takes the shape of the things that push against it. In Paul's language, it is transformed. When I squeeze the clay in my hand, it changes its shape to fit my fingers. When I press this golf ball against it, the clay accepts the shape of the ball. The same is true of a building block. The one way in which you and I are like the modeling clay is that we are influenced by our surroundings. We don't change our shape, but we do change the way we talk, the way we act, and even the way we think. Our lives are molded by the people we are with, the books we read, and the things we

31

do. That is why Paul warns us not to be conformed to this world. Just as the clay is changed by what comes up against it, so are we. What is the model for your life?

This presents a problem because we can't step off the world to avoid contact with others. Nor can we hide someplace to avoid all people who might lead us astray. In fact, we are supposed to be near such people so that we can help them. But what if, instead of our changing them, they change us?

Paul has a solution. He says we are to conform to God's will. We are changed by whatever is nearest to us and most important to us. Christ can be the nearest to us because He has come to live among us. We cannot become God, but God has become man. Christ is present in our lives. Your baptism assures you that you have put on Christ. In Him we receive the blessings of God.

Christ gave us these gifts when He died on the cross; so let's be transformed by the cross [*press cross into the clay*]. The cross in our lives changes us. It assures us that we are forgiven. It gives us the reason and the power to serve God. The cross is impressed into your life when you hear of Christ and believe in Him. The Holy Spirit uses the message of Christ's life to transform our lives. Amen.

A Tool for Every Job

The Word

Having gifts that differ according to the grace given to us, let us use them: if prophecy, in proportion to our faith; if service, in our serving; he who teaches, in his teaching; he who exhorts, in his exhortation; he who contributes, in liberality; he who gives aid, with zeal; he who does acts of mercy, with cheerfulness. Romans 12:6-8 (From the Epistle for the Second Sunday After Epiphany)

The World

Scissors, kitchen knife, razor blade, and cookie cutter

If I asked you to bring me something with which to cut, what would you bring me? You might offer me these scissors. That would be fine if I wanted to cut paper or cloth. But what if I wanted to peel an apple? The scissors wouldn't do the job very well. Then you might bring me a knife. The knife will cut many things, but what if I wanted to shave? Maybe I could shave with a knife; I'd rather not try. For that I need a razor blade. I could cut many other things with this razor blade. But what if I wanted to cut out cookies? None of the cutters we have here would work well. For that I would need a cookie cutter.

The point of showing you all these everyday tools is to remind you that in one sense they all do the same thing. They all cut. Yet they all serve different purposes.

In the same way Paul reminds us that we all have the same job to do. Because Christ has redeemed us we are to glorify His name and serve in His kingdom. Everyone of us is to use the grace and the power of Christ in our everyday life.

But that doesn't mean that we all do exactly the same thing. Just as all of these tools cut, so also all Christians serve. But just as each tool cuts in a different way, so also we Christians serve in different ways.

Paul lists some of the different ways in which we serve. Some can prophecy, that is, proclaim the Word of God. Some can minister, that is, serve God's people. Some can teach, and to that we might add that some can learn. Some can exhort, that is, correct those who are wrong. Some can give, not only money but also time and ability. Some can rule, that is, use their authority in a God-pleasing way. Some can show mercy.

We could add more to the list, but you get the idea that there are many ways to serve God. We have a pastor of this congregation. Others serve as teachers and officers. Many serve as witnesses for Christ. Many support the church with offerings. You children also serve. You serve by learning, by obeying your parents, by bringing your offerings, by inviting others to church and Sunday school. In a congregation such as ours we need many different kinds of servants, but we all serve the same Lord.

Do you know how you serve? If you do, then serve with joy. If you don't know how to serve, look to the Savior and see what He has done for you. Then you can think of a way to serve. Amen.

Whose Side Are You On?

The Word

Do not be overcome by evil, but overcome evil with good. Romans 12:21 (From the Epistle for the Third Sunday After Epiphany)

The World

A board from a child's game which has spaces for markers to advance. For markers use red and blue paper with tape on back so the board can be held upright.

You know how to play a game like this. If the player who has the blue marker spins a four, he advances his marker four spaces, like this. Then the other player spins. He advances his marker like this. If two of your friends were playing and you came to watch, you wouldn't have to ask who was red and who was blue. It would be easy to tell by watching which player moved which marker. If you saw me move the blue marker, you would know that the blue was mine and the red belonged to the other player.

In the same way people can tell whose side you are on by the way you talk and act. Take, for example, the problem of good and evil. All of us face many decisions each day that involve a choice between doing what is right and what is wrong. When you make those decisions, you show which side you are on. If you do what is right, you are on the side of good. If you do what is wrong, you are on the side of evil.

Paul tells us not to let evil overcome us, but to overcome evil. On our playing board it would look like this. Blue is good and red is evil. When you do that which is good you would move the blue marker forward. When you choose evil, you move the red marker forward. We all say we want the good to win in our lives. But if someone else were watching you move the markers in your life, would he know whose side you are on?

That's where Jesus comes into our lives. He, too, is watching the game. Like others who watch, Jesus gives help and advice. He helps us avoid evil so that the evil marker won't be advanced. He tells us to do that which is good so that the good marker can advance.

But Jesus does more than give advice. He gets into the game. Because He is holy, all of His actions move the good marker ahead. But instead of having His own marker, He lets you move your marker forward when He spins. That's another way of saying that you get credit for the good that He does. When Jesus is in your game, the good marker always wins. He puts it to the finish line. Evil does not overcome you, but Jesus overcomes evil and gives you the victory.

You know who won that game, don't you? Jesus did. But He won it in your life; so you share in the victory. Amen.

Pay Back What You Borrow

The Word

Owe no one anything, except to love one another; for he who loves his neighbor has fulfilled the Law. Romans 13:8 (From the Epistle for the Fourth Sunday After Epiphany)

The World

A dollar bill and three marbles

If I asked to borrow a dollar from you, would you loan it to me? Maybe some of you have a dollar. Here's one. We'll pretend that you loaned it to me. If I borrowed it, then I should return it. So now it is time for me to pay you back. But instead of giving you a dollar, I'll give you these three marbles. Is that fair? I'm sure you wouldn't think so. If I borrowed a dollar, then I must return a dollar. Of course, if I had borrowed three marbles, then I would have returned three marbles. You must always give back what you borrow.

In our Bible text St. Paul also talks about owing and paying back. It says: "Owe no one anything, except to love one another; for he who loves his neighbor has fulfilled the Law." Paul tells you that you should pay back everything you owe. But he says that you will always owe love. You can never pay back all the love you owe to others, but you should always be giving it back.

Let's look at it this way. God gives you love in Christ. There is no way to measure the amount of love God gives you. It is so much love that Christ died for you. It is so much love that all of your sins are forgiven. It is so much love that God will keep you with Him forever.

God has given us this love. It is not a loan. But He has told us to use the love by loving Him and loving all other people. In a sense you can say you are returning His love when you love God. God has also said that you can return the love He has given you by giving it to others. In the same way I could loan you a dime and tell you to return it to your mother because I wanted her to have it. We can give God's love to all people because He wants all people to have it.

But are you returning the love God has given to you? Remember how great that love is. It is beyond measure. Are you returning that kind of love? Or are you returning marbles when you received dollars?

You return God's love to Him by worshiping Him, by serving Him, and by giving His love to others. You give His love to others by treating them as you would like to be treated. You speak kind words to them. You help them when they need help. Sometimes it may be hard to love people who do not seem to want to be loved. But remember that God has given you love. You can pass the love on to others. Amen.

Let's Check Your Uniform

The Word

Put on then, as God's chosen ones, holy and beloved, compassion, kindness, lowliness, meekness, and patience, forbearing one another and, if one has a complaint against another, forgiving each other; as the Lord has forgiven you, so you also must forgive. Colossians 3:12-14 (From the Epistle for the Fifth Sunday After Epiphany)

The World

Sailor hat, gun and holster set, baseball mitt

Do you know what a man wearing this hat [*show sailor hat*] would be? Of course he would be a sailor. But what if the same man also wore this holster and this mitt? That would be confusing. The hat would make him look like a sailor, the holster would make him look like a cowboy, and the mitt would make him look like a ballplayer. If he had on all three, he would just confuse us.

We might also confuse people regarding our Christian faith. Paul tells us to put on certain things as if they were a uniform. He says: "Put on then, as God's chosen ones, holy and beloved, compassion, kindness, lowliness, meekness, and patience, forbearing one another and, if one has a complaint against another, forgiving each other; as the Lord has forgiven you, so you also must forgive." Notice that Paul says the uniform should be worn by the elect of God. God has chosen you. For proof that He has chosen you, remember your baptism. God chose you in Baptism by giving you the new life in Christ. He doesn't ask you to provide your own uniform. Christ has given you all the things that are listed. But He does ask you to wear them. Let's check your uniform.

Do you have mercy and kindness for other people — not only for those who are kind and merciful to you but to all people? Can others see your kindness? your mercy? Do you wear it always, or do you have it tucked away some place just for inspections?

Next we check for humility and meekness. Do these qualities show in your life? Do you show humility when you win games? How is your meekness when you bring home a good report card?

A Christian is also to wear longsuffering and forbearance; which means you are to be patient. Even if the rest of the family is slow, even if your little brothers and sisters annoy you, you are to be patient. Is that a part of your uniform? Do your little brothers and sisters see your patience?

Your uniform includes forgiveness to others because you are forgiven, love to others because you are loved by Christ.

Are all of these things a part of your daily appearance? Then you wear the uniform of a Christian. Or are you like the man with the hat, holster, and mitt? Do you have some of the Christian uniform plus items from another team such as anger, pride, or jealousy? A mixed uniform is confusing. To be on the safe side go to Christ each day and ask for a full uniform of His righteousness. Then you will always be in proper uniform. Amen.

Turn the Lights On in Your Life

The Word

And we have the prophetic Word made more sure. You will do well to pay attention to this as to a lamp shining in a dark place, until the day dawns and the morning star rises in your hearts. 2 Peter 1:19 (From the Epistle for the Transfiguration)

The World

A flashlight with batteries removed at the beginning of the sermon

What a day it must have been for Peter when he saw Jesus, Moses, and Elijah transfigured! It must have been like a bright light in his life. Yet he tells us that we have something even more sure and more important — we have the Bible. Maybe the Bible doesn't always seem so wonderful to you. If not, it might be because you have forgotten how the power of Scripture works. This illustration will remind you:

See this flashlight battery. It is a new one; so you know that it has power in it. The power was put in it at a factory somewhere. Do you know how to get the power out of the battery? You can't open a battery and pour the power out like gasoline. You can't squeeze the power out like water from a sponge.

The only way to get the power out of the battery is to connect it with something that can use its power. This flashlight won't work now because it has no batteries. But put the batteries in it and look, you have light. The flashlight and the batteries were meant for each other. Neither can make light by itself, but together there is light.

In the same way there is power in the Bible. God put the power into the Scriptures. The Word of God contains the power of salvation because it tells us that Christ has given His life for us. Do you know how to get the power from the Bible? You can't receive the power by holding the Bible or by using it as a table decoration or even by defending it.

The power of the Bible comes out when we read it. We are like the flashlight without batteries. We are in the spiritual darkness of sin. But when the power of the Bible is added to our lives, we are changed from darkness to light. The Holy Spirit uses the message of Christ's forgiveness, His honor and glory which we see in the Transfiguration, as a power to change our lives.

God has made the Bible for us. He has put the power of Christ into it. The power is for each of us. When you receive that power, it is a great day for you. Let every day be that great day. Amen.

The Way to Aim a Life

The Word

Do you not know that in a race all the runners compete, but only one receives the prize? So run that you may obtain it. 1 Corinthians 9:24 (From the Epistle for Septuagesima Sunday)

The World

A toy rifle with sights

Most of you boys probably play with guns. Maybe you girls do too. But do you know how to aim a gun? If you are pretending to shoot, you don't have to be careful about aiming because you always hit what you aim at when you pretend. But to aim a gun to hit something, you must line up three things. First the sight which is close to your eye, then the sight which is at the end of the barrel, then the target. If you line up only two of the three, the gun is not aimed.

In the same way you have to set the sights of your life by lining up three things. St. Paul tells us that we are to run a race so that we will win. A race is similar to sighting a rifle. You have to know where you start, where you are going, and how you get there. You sight your life by these same three things.

First, where are you now? You have to consider your present situation in life, what you have and what you need, your weaknesses and your good points. In all of this you will see that you need God's help. These facts are this part of the sight [*point to sight near your eye*]; that's where the bullet is before you shoot.

Next, where are you going? What is your first goal in life? After that? And after that? Is it just your final goal to be with God? Or do you want to be with Him now? It is important that you know all the goals of your life. Too many people just aim their life at nothing and hit it. Your goals are the target at which you aim; that's where the bullet goes.

Now to line up where you are now with where you want to go we have to use this middle sight [*point to sight at end of barrel*]; that's where the bullet goes on its way to the target. What way will you go to hit your target? If your goal is to be with God, there is only one possible sight for you to line up your life. That is the cross of Christ. To line your life up on Christ means to see His life and your life together. Like the two sights, they must be seen together. You then see that Christ was born to be your Savior. He died to pay for your sins. Because He lives, you will live also. You are frequently told of these things so that you may believe them and see Christ in your life.

Only by the cross can you get from your place as a sinner to the presence of God. Only by sighting your life on the cross can you be assured that you have the love and help of Christ at all times during your life. Your life may frequently get off target; because you upset things at this end [*sight near the eye*] by your sin. But always come back to the way of Christ by lining up on the cross again in repentance, and you will be back on target. Amen.

The Advantage of Weakness

The Word

If I must boast, I will boast of the things that show my weakness.
2 Corinthians 11:30 (From the Epistle for Sexagesima Sunday)

The World

A piece of kite string and a piece of cord about the length of a cord on a draw drape

When most people brag, they brag about how great they are. In the Bible reading the apostle Paul brags about how weak he is. That seems like a strange way to boast. But Paul had a good reason for being glad that he knew he was weak. When we understand our own weaknesses, we also have a reason to be glad. Let's illustrate it.

Suppose two men are on top of a burning building. There is no way for them to get down. One of the men has a piece of cord this size just long enough to reach to the ground. But he is not sure if the cord is strong enough to hold him. He tries to test it by pulling on it. It seems strong. So he starts climbing down the cord. But it is not strong enough. The cord breaks, and the man is killed in the fall.

The other man on the burning building had only a long piece of string. He knew that the string was not strong enough to hold him. See. I can break it in my hands. He thought there was no way for him to escape. Just as he had given up hope a hook-and-ladder truck came. The ladder was extended to the roof. The man was saved. Now he was glad

45

that he had had only a weak piece of string. That way he had to wait for help instead of trying to save himself. The weak string saved his life; if he had had the stronger cord, he might also have tried to climb down it.

In the same way if you think that you are good enough to save your own soul, you won't look for help from anyone else. Many people think that they are good. They have tried hard to obey God's law. They have helped their neighbors and followed the Golden Rule. Therefore, they trust their good works to save them. But no one is good enough to save himself. We are all sinners, and the wages of sin is death.

When we realize that we are not good enough to save ourselves, we are like the man with the small string. We have to wait for someone else to save us. Christ is that someone. He has come and has paid the price of our sin. He has saved us from eternal death. Because we are weak, we have to depend on Him. Every day we need to turn to Him for forgiveness. Every day we need His love and help. That is why we can be glad that we are weak. Our weakness serves a good purpose if it drives us to Christ to receive His help. When we know Christ and His strength, we can brag of our own weakness. Amen.

The Test of Use

The Word

If I speak in the tongues of men and of angels, but have not love, I am a noisy gong or a clanging cymbal. And if I have prophetic powers, and understand all mysteries and all knowledge, and if I have all faith, so as to remove mountains, but have not love, I am nothing. 1 Corinthians 13:1-2 (From the Epistle for Quinquagesima Sunday)

The World

A ball-point pen with ink tube and ball point removed, writing paper, ruler, and eraser

It's time for a test at school. Don't start worrying about it. We will pretend that I have to take it instead of you. The teacher has told me to bring a pen, paper, ruler, and an eraser. And I am well prepared. See: pen, paper, ruler, eraser. We're all ready for the test. The teacher puts the questions on the chalkboard. I start to write the first answer. But — my ball-point pen won't write. It looks like a good pen. It has a nice clip. It is a pretty color. But it has no ink tube and no ball point. The most important part of the pen is missing. So I am really not prepared after all.

In the same way Paul tells us what is the most important thing we need to be a Christian. If you remember, don't tell anyone. If you don't remember, what do you think is the most important thing about being a Christian?

You might say it is important to belong to a church, but that's not the most important. It is important to go to church and to support the work of the church, but something else is more important. It is important to obey your parents, not to cheat in school, and to get along with your friends. But those things don't make you a Christian.

Paul tells you that the most important thing is love. You must receive the love Christ gives to you. That love is not something you can buy or earn. It is a love that is given to you because God is love.

The Christian not only receives this love. He also gives love to others. If we look like good church members, if we go to Sunday school every week, if everyone thinks we are good people, but we do not have love, then we are missing the whole purpose of Christianity.

A ball-point pen without a ball point is worthless, and so is religion without love. Love is the basis of our relationship with God and it is the basis of our relationship with one another. Your faith is ready for the test when you have received love and when you are able to give love.

Sometimes we are unable to love others. Sometimes we feel our love growing weak. Those are the times to go back to the Source of love. Hear again how God first loved you and gave Jesus to be your Savior. Receive the love He gives so freely; then pass it on to others. Amen.

Have You Used Your Grace Today?

The Word

Working together with Him, then, we entreat you not to accept the grace of God in vain. 2 Corinthians 6:1 (From the Epistle for the First Sunday in Lent)

The World

A bottle of pills with instructions on the label

Here is a bottle of pills from a doctor. The instructions say, "Take one pill four times a day." Let's pretend that these pills are for you. Your mother tells you that you are big enough to remember to take your own pills. So she puts the bottle into the cabinet and tells you to take one pill four times a day.

I hope you wouldn't do this but suppose that after breakfast you went to the cabinet, took one pill out of the bottle, like this, put the pill in your pocket, and went off to school. At lunch time you take another pill from the bottle and put it in your pocket. The same thing after dinner and at bedtime. In a sense, you took the pill each time. But you didn't take it as you were supposed to. The pills would do you no good if you took them and put them in your pocket. We could say that you were taking the pills in vain. That means that you were not using them as you should.

In our Bible reading Paul tells us not to receive the grace of God in vain. God's grace is the gift that He has given you through Christ. We deserve to be punished for our sins, but

God forgives us through Christ. That is grace. We deserve to be far away from God, but Christ has come to us. That is grace. Each time you hear what Christ has done for you, you receive God's grace. But are you receiving it as we pretended you took those pills? Are you just hearing about grace but not receiving the blessings it offers you? That would be receiving the grace of God in vain.

Here are some ways in which you might receive the grace of God in vain. You might hear that your sins are forgiven and still worry about your guilt. That would be receiving God's grace in vain because we are forgiven by His grace. Or you might hear of Christ's love for you and then be afraid of all the problems which you have. That would be hearing God's grace in vain, because His grace helps us through our problems. Or you might receive God's grace and then say, "I can sin all I want to; because Jesus will forgive me." That would be using God's grace in vain because His grace not only forgives us but gives us strength to fight against temptation and sin.

There are many other ways in which we can use God's grace in vain. But more important, we use God's grace the right way when we apply the message of Christ to our daily lives. Just as the pills have to be swallowed to help you, so also the grace of God must be applied to your life. You can't just hear it, but you must hear it and say, "That's what I need." And Christ gives it to you. Amen.

How High Can You Reach?

The Word

Finally, brethren, we beseech and exhort you in the Lord Jesus, that as you learned from us how you ought to live and to please God, just as you are doing, you do so more and more. 1 Thessalonians 4:1 (From the Epistle for the Second Sunday in Lent)

The World

A child about four years old

Did you hear what we read from the Bible? Paul said you are to please God. Each day you are to do more and more to serve Him. You may remember that in other places the Bible says that no one can please God because all people are sinners. It even says that our righteous deeds, that is, the good things we do for Him, are like filthy rags in His sight. It seems as though there is no use trying to please God if we can't do it.

But remember that Paul asked us to do these good things in Christ. He knows that we can't do them by ourselves, but that is not an excuse for not serving God. Christ has come to help us. Let me show you how His help works. Jim, would you please come and help me.

Jim, you stand right beside me. Now, can you touch my hand? That was easy, wasn't it? Can you reach up and touch the cross I am wearing? You just barely made it. Let's try once more: Can you touch the top of my head? You can't do it, can you? Jim must feel as we do when we are told to serve

51

God and we know we can't do it.

But you see, Jim, you can touch the top of my head. [*Stoop down beside the child.*] It is easy, if I help you. We should all remember that Christ has also helped us. He stooped down to become a man and to take our place in obeying the Law and in dying for our sins. When Paul tells us to serve God, he tells us to do it in Christ. We can do it because Christ helps us do it.

But that's not all. After Christ died, He arose from the dead and now rules all the earth. When He arose, He gave us a new life also. He lifts us up from the life of sin [*pick up the child*] by forgiving our sins and by giving us His power to fight against sin. Now, Jim, can you touch the top of my head? Sure you can — as long as I hold you up. Remember that Christ also holds you up. When you want to serve God, first go to Christ and ask Him to help. He will stoop down and pick you up. You can then serve God with Christ's help. Amen.

Keep Your Eyes Wide Open

The Word

For once you were darkness, but now you are light in the Lord; walk as children of light. Ephesians 5:8 (From the Epistle for the Third Sunday in Lent)

The World

A second-grade child, a blindfold, some writing paper on a clipboard, and a felt-tip marking pencil

[*Call the child to stand beside you to help.*] Debbie, I'm going to ask you to do something I know you can do. Please write your name on this piece of paper. [*As the child takes the clipboard and pen, place blindfold over her eyes.*] Now you go ahead and write your name.

[*After the name is written, take the clipboard and remove blindfold.*] I thought you could write your name better than that, Debbie. But it wasn't fair, was it? Why don't you do it again — this time without the blindfold. [*Return the board and pen.*]

That's better, Debbie. Thank you, you may go back to your place now. That little experiment proved that a person can write better without a blindfold than with one. I am sure you already knew that. But sometimes we wear spiritual blindfolds. Debbie knew how to write her name, but she couldn't see to do it. We also often know what we should do and what we should not do. But that doesn't mean that we do the right things and avoid the wrong things. Our spiritual blindfolds prevent us from doing what we know we should do.

St. Paul puts it this way: "For once you were darkness, but now you are light in the Lord; walk as children of light." We are in darkness each time we refuse to use the power which we have. We often shut our eyes to the opportunities to serve God by putting on spiritual blindfolds. Some spiritual blindfolds are: selfishness, hate, laziness, the refusal to learn God's Word, prejudice, and jealousy. When we try to serve God by looking through these things, we are spiritually blindfolded. We can do nothing right.

But Christ has removed our spiritual blindfolds from us. He has died to pay for the sins that have made us live in darkness. We do not have to hide from the fact of our own sins. Instead we go to Christ and ask for His forgiveness. He assures us that He has forgiven us because He died to pay for our sins. Believe in Christ, and you can walk as a child of the Light. We walk in light when we know that we are saved by Christ and now live with Him.

Live in His light! Ask Him for guidance and strength. Each time sin comes to blindfold you, turn to your Savior to have the blindfold removed. Amen.

Ask Before You Promise

The Word

Tell me, you who desire to be under Law, do you not hear the Law? Galatians 4:21 (From the Epistle for the Fourth Sunday in Lent)

The World

A sealed envelope with paper inside

I need someone to do a chore for me. Would you help me? The job that I need done is explained in this envelope. Would one of you offer to do it for me? Better be careful. What if you offered to do this job without opening the envelope? You might find that you couldn't do what I asked. The job might be to build a building or to swim the ocean. You couldn't do that.

I'll open the envelope and tell you what the job is. The instructions say, "Please carry the box from my garage to the kitchen. Thank you." You could do that job for me, couldn't you? That's the kind of job you do for your mother and father every day. Would all of you agree to do this chore for me?

You had better be careful again. The instructions do not say how big the box is or what is in it. What if you promised to do this chore for me and then found that the box was five feet wide and the kitchen door is only three feet wide? What if the box is filled with bricks and weighs 500 pounds? You couldn't carry that. You should ask about a task before you promise to do it. Maybe you wouldn't be able to do what you promised.

In the same way Paul warns us not to think that we can be saved by the Law until we know what the Law says. He says: "Tell me, you who desire to be under Law, do you not hear the Law?" To be under the Law means to be willing to keep all of God's law. Each time you think that God loves you because you are good, you are putting yourself under the Law. Each time you think that God owes you a favor because you have obeyed some of His commandments, you are putting yourself under the Law. Each time you think that you are better than someone else because the other person has broken more commandments than you, you are putting yourself under the Law.

Before you volunteer to be judged by the Law, you had better know what the Law says. It not only says not to kill or to hate anyone, it also says to love all people. It not only says not to worship idols, it also says to keep God first in your life at all times. The Law says that you must be perfect — as perfect as God is.

But Christ has volunteered to keep the Law for us. Because He kept His promise, we don't have to be under the Law. Instead, we can be under His Gospel. The Gospel tells you your sins are forgiven. It tells you that you live by grace. Believe in Christ and live under the Gospel. Amen.

How to Get Well Soon

The Word

How much more shall the blood of Christ, who through the eternal Spirit offered Himself without blemish to God, purify your conscience from dead works to serve the living God. Hebrews 9:14 (From the Epistle for the Fifth Sunday in Lent)

The World

A get-well card and either a prescription from a doctor or a bottle of prescriptive medicine

Most of you have probably been sick at least once. You may have received a card like this one. It says: [*read card*]. It is always nice to receive get-well cards when you are sick. It shows that others are thinking about you. It cheers you up and helps pass the time away. But you know that the get-well cards don't make you well. If all you need is for someone to tell you to get well, then you really aren't sick. You can't just tell the measles to go away or a broken leg to quit hurting.

But here is something else that you might receive when you are sick. It does help you get well. It is a prescription. You know that this comes from a doctor. The prescription doesn't just say, "Get well." It gives you something that helps make you well.

Sin is also a sickness. It is a sickness that destroys life. A cure for sin sickness has to remove the guilt of past sins and help us fight against future sins. But that is a difficult cure. We can do a lot of talking about sin. We can say that we are not as bad as others. We can point out the fact that we have done many good things. We can even tell one another not to worry about sin — if anyone gets to heaven, surely we will. All of this kind of talk is like a "get well spiritually" card. It sounds nice but doesn't do much good.

We need a prescription for our sin sickness. God has given such a prescription. He saw our guilt and sent His Son to be our Savior. Jesus didn't come just to tell us to stop sinning. Nor did He come just to give us God's best wishes. He came to die for our sin. He went to the cause of our problems. By paying for our sins He removed our guilt. By using the power which He gives us, we can fight against sin.

The writer to the Hebrews reminds us how the Old Testament people made sacrifices to pay for sins. That was like a get-well card. It reminded them that they were sick and that they needed help. But if it helped them just to be reminded that they would have help, how much more it will help to know that their sins are actually paid for. The prescription for our sin sickness has been filled by Christ. Let's use it by believing it. Amen.

Help That Looks Helpless

The Word

But [Christ] emptied Himself, taking the form of a servant, being born in the likeness of men. And being found in human form He humbled Himself and became obedient unto death, even death on a cross. Philippians 2:7-8 (From the Epistle for Palm Sunday)

The World

A waste basket filled with assorted waste paper, including several used envelopes and a 20-dollar bill

You know what is in a waste basket. Just old waste paper. Here is a newspaper from last week, some old envelopes, used napkins, all of it just waste paper. The whole basketful is ready to be taken out and burned. Here is another piece of paper [*show 20-dollar bill*]. But this is not waste paper. It is worth 20 dollars. We keep this kind of paper carefully tucked away in our billfolds or in a cash register.

Suppose that this 20-dollar bill were in an old envelope [*place it in an envelope from the waste basket*] and it were accidentally dropped into the basket with all the waste paper [*drop envelope into basket and mix up paper*]. Would you burn this basket of waste paper now? Of course, you would not. Even though you can't see the 20-dollar bill, you know it is in the basket. The rest of the paper is still worthless, but it is protected from burning by the 20-dollar bill in the basket with it.

In one way you and I are like this waste paper. Because

we have disobeyed God we can no longer fulfill the purpose for which He created us. Our lives away from God made us waste people, ready to be destroyed. But Christ is like the 20-dollar bill. He came to live with us. Our text says: "[Christ] emptied Himself, taking the form of a servant, being born in the likeness of men." As the 20-dollar bill looks like the rest of the waste paper when it is in an envelope so also Christ, the true Son of God, became one of us.

By becoming one of us, Jesus accepted all the problems of our lives. The greatest problem of our lives is death — the destruction which we deserve because of our sin. That was our problem, not Jesus' problem. Yet He was willing to take our problem. He died for us. Paul says, "Being found in human form He humbled Himself and became obedient unto death, even death on a cross."

Our Help looked very helpless when He died. But He arose from the dead and remains with us. We are protected because He died for our guilt and He remains with us with His love and grace. Because He is with us we are no longer waste people separated from God by our sins. He has taken our destruction, our death, and He has given us His life. With Christ living in us, we can do the things for which God created us. We can love God and serve Him. We can love other people and serve them. With Christ in us, we are no longer in a waste basket waiting for destruction. We have been rescued! Amen.

Help Where It Counts

The Word

Surely He has borne our griefs and carried our sorrows; yet we esteemed Him stricken, smitten by God, and afflicted. But He was wounded for our transgressions, He was bruised for our iniquities; upon Him was the chastisement that made us whole, and with His stripes we are healed. Isaiah 53:4-5 (From the Epistle for Good Friday)

The World

A nutcracker, several nuts in the shells, a bolt longer than the width of a finger but short enough to fit in the jaws of the nutcracker

Most of you boys and girls have probably helped your mother use one of these [*hold up nutcracker*]. It is easy to operate. See! You put the nut in the jaws of the nutcracker and squeeze hard. The shell of the nut cracks wide open. Just imagine how much pressure the nutcracker puts on the nut to break it like that. Would you be willing to put your finger in the jaws of the nutcracker and let me squeeze as hard as I did when I broke the nut shell? Sounds as if it would hurt, doesn't it? Do you think it would break your finger?

I'm not afraid to put my finger in the nutcracker and squeeze. Look. [*Place the bolt into the jaws of the nutcracker to hold it open. Now put your finger beside the bolt in the jaws and squeeze.*] See, it didn't hurt my finger a bit. Of course, you can see why. All of the pressure of the nutcracker was on the bolt. My finger was perfectly safe because the bolt held the jaws of the nutcracker wide open.

You don't have to put your finger in a nutcracker to be hurt. We have many other pains in life. Isaiah describes some of our pains in the Bible reading. He says we have griefs and sorrows. He says we are to be wounded for our transgressions, that is, our sins. He says we should be bruised for our iniquities; again that means our evil doing. He says that we need to be chastised and whipped. All of these things describe the punishment we deserve as sinners. It is a punishment much worse than putting your finger in a nutcracker because it is more than physical punishment. It is the punishment of being separated from God.

Isaiah describes all of those pains, but he does not say that you and I will actually suffer them. In fact, we won't. We don't have to fear such punishment because Christ has taken them for us. He is like the bolt that took all the pressure of the nutcracker and protected my finger. Christ has taken the punishment of sin so that we do not have to bear it. Listen to Isaiah describe it: "Surely He has borne our griefs and carried our sorrows; yet we esteemed Him stricken, smitten by God, and afflicted. But He was wounded for our transgressions, He was bruised for our iniquities; upon Him was the chastisement that made us whole, and with His stripes we are healed."

The message of Good Friday is that Christ has taken our place on the cross. He stood in the jaws of death for us. When it is our time to die, we won't be alone. Christ is there. He has removed the punishment of death. Amen.

Easter Is a Fresh Drink of Water

The Word

Your boasting is not good. Do you not know that a little leaven leavens the whole lump? Cleanse out the old leaven that you may be a new lump, as you really are unleavened. 1 Corinthians 5:6-7a (From the Epistle for Easter Sunday)

The World

A glass of water and a piece of dirt (Note: A blossom from an Easter lily will be needed next Sunday.)

What does this glass of water make you think about? Notice how fresh and clear the water is. When I move the glass, the water almost seems to sparkle. Even if you weren't thirsty before I showed you the water, I imagine that you're getting thirsty now. Just the sight of cool, fresh water in a clean, clear glass makes most of us want a drink. In fact, you might like a drink right now. Would you? Sure, I'll be glad to give you this water, but first . . . [*crumble dirt into the glass*]. Anybody who wants to drink this water may come and get it.

But I'm not thirsty any more, are you? Just one little piece of dirt ruined that nice glass of water. The sight of clean water made us thirsty, but the sight of dirty water makes us decide to wait for a drink. I don't even feel thirsty when I look at dirty water.

In the same way Easter can make people anxious to be near God. When we show the true meaning of Easter, it is like showing a glass of water to a thirsty person. Easter is an oasis of life in a world of death. It is a glass of forgiveness to a person dying of the thirst of guilt. Easter has a clear, direct, simple message. It says that Christ who died now lives and that all who should die may live through Him. Isn't it wonderful to hear about Easter? How wonderful to know that new life is offered to us!

But in our Bible reading Paul warns us that we can ruin Easter for ourselves and others by adding old troubles to the new joy we have in Christ. Dirt ruined the water. We can also add things to Easter that ruin the message of Christ's resurrection. Christ's victory over death is a fresh glass of water, but when we are still afraid of death, we add a lump of dirt to the water. Easter assures us our sins are forgiven because Christ won the victory over sin. We add a lump of dirt when we refuse to forgive others. Easter is a message of hope because Christ's resurrection assures us that we, too, will be raised from the dead. We add a lump of dirt when we show we have no hope.

Let's celebrate Easter without adding the cares and problems of the world to it. This doesn't mean that we just ignore these things for a while and then go back to the problems of life next week. Easter gives us a way to live with the cares and problems of life. Christ's resurrection assures us that we will not be destroyed by the evils of this life. The final victory is a victory over death itself. Amen.

Leftover Easter

The Word

This is the victory that overcomes the world, our faith. Who is it that overcomes the world but he who believes that Jesus is the Son of God? 1 John 5:4b-5 (From the Epistle for the First Sunday After Easter)

The World

A dried Easter lily blossom from last Sunday's altar

I want to show you something beautiful [*dried flower*]. At least it was beautiful. Last Sunday this flower was on our altar. Then it was fresh and beautiful. The beautiful, white blossom that had come from a dried-up bulb reminded us of the living Christ, who had died three days before.

But look at the flower now. Then it was fresh; now it is stale. Then it was white; now it is brown, and not a pretty brown at that. This flower is an Easter leftover.

What else do you have left over from Easter? Maybe you had new clothes last Sunday. If so, I am sure they lasted better than this flower. But they, too, have lost their magic of newness. By now I imagine you've eaten most of the Easter eggs and candy. But what about the happiness and the joy you had last week? Remember what a thrill it was to hear the message of the angels, "He is risen"? Remember the blessing which we received when Christ destroyed death?

What has happened to that joy which you received last week? This flower represented our living joy then. Does it also represent our faith this week — that is, a wilted and stale faith? If so, we missed the real joy of the Resurrection victory.

Jesus' victory over death is different from all other victories. Other victories are followed by more battles and possible defeats. History tells us that when a country wins one war, it will face another. When a ball team wins one game, it is a victory, but they have to face another team soon. Even a World Series victory is good for only about six months. Then the winning team starts over with all the other teams. When you recover from a sickness, it seems like a victory. But that victory can be forgotten because there are other problems.

But the victory of Easter lasts. Jesus did not just win a battle over the Pharisees who demanded His death or over the soldiers who nailed Him to the cross. His victory was over death — all death, including ours. Today's Epistle promises us a victory that overcomes the whole world. That is a lasting victory. We have this victory in our faith — faith that Jesus Christ is the Son of God. Such faith receives the grace Christ has offered to all people. Our faith is a faith that wins because it trusts in a Savior who won. His victory wasn't just a temporary victory to be followed by another battle. He lives never to die again. His resurrection is just as true today as it was the first Easter morning because He still lives today. Easter leftovers need not be warmed over, worn out, or wilted. In Christ we have a victory that is new every day. Amen.

A Pattern for Life

The Word

For to this you have been called, because Christ also suffered for you, leaving you an example, that you should follow in His steps. 1 Peter 2:21 (From the Epistle for the Second Sunday After Easter)

The World

A simple picture of Christ, the Good Shepherd (perhaps from a Sunday school leaflet), a sheet of typing paper on a clipboard, and a felt-tip marking pen

This picture of Christ all of you recognize. It is Christ the Good Shepherd. Do you think you could draw this picture? I'll show you how easy it is to draw it. [*Place picture on clipboard under typing paper. Trace outline of the picture.*] See? I'm not an artist, but I can draw the picture.

Of course, you can see why it is easy for me to draw the picture. The original picture is under the paper, and I am tracing it. That is the easy way to draw. But notice that the paper has to touch the picture in order to trace. If the picture were several inches away from the paper, I wouldn't be able to trace it.

In the same way we can't be far away from Christ and still see Him as the Good Shepherd in our lives. St. Peter tells us that we have been called to follow Christ. He is an example for us, and we are to follow in His steps. This means that our life is to be patterned after His, in much the same way as I drew a picture by tracing from another picture.

If our lives are to be like Christ's life, we must first of all see His life. We must see that He is our Savior, the Son of God, who also became man so that He could die for our sins. We have to see the love and mercy He has given to us. We have to see how His death takes away our guilt and His resurrection gives us the power of eternal life.

All of this is wonderful to see. But too often we see this as something far away — a picture on a wall. But if He is to be our example, we must be near Him — near enough that our lives can be copied from His. When Peter tells us to follow in His steps, he does not mean that we should follow at a great distance, where we can see only His footprints. But we are to be near Him, where we can see Him and follow Him. This is possible because He has remained near us. Even though He was taken away from us when He was killed, He returned on the third day and lives with us now.

When you feel afraid and lonely, when you are weak and tempted, remember the picture of the Good Shepherd. Remember how He has come to you in your baptism and remains with you by the power of the Holy Spirit. Amen.

Till the Day Iron Floats

The Word

Maintain good conduct among the Gentiles, so that in case they speak against you as wrongdoers, they may see your good deeds and glorify God on the day of visitation. 1 Peter 2:12 (From the Epistle for the Third Sunday After Easter)

The World

A key, a glass of water, and a plastic fishing bobber (the kind that hooks onto the line)

What do you think will happen when I put this metal key in this glass of water? Most of you probably think that the key will sink to the bottom. But I think it will stay near the top. We could discuss what will happen, and maybe even argue about it. But instead, let's try it. [*Fasten the key to the bobber and drop it in the glass.*]

See! I told you the key would stay near the top. Of course, you didn't know that I would hook it to a float. But that's what makes the difference. The key can stay near the top if the bobber does the floating and the key just rides along.

In the same way it seems impossible for us to do all the things Peter tells us to do in our Bible reading. He tells us that we should obey all the laws of both God and man. We are supposed to love all people — even the mean ones. We are supposed to bear our troubles without griping about it. But it seems impossible for us to do all those tasks. We are human, and it is more natural for people to complain, to dislike one another, and to break the laws of God and man, just as it is natural for iron to sink in water.

But the iron could float when it had something to hold it up. We also can do the things St. Peter requests if we have someone to hold us up. And we have Christ, who in His life and death came down to the bottom where we had sunk, but who now by His resurrection from the dead has returned to the top where we should be. And He lifts us up with Him. His resurrection tells us not only that we will live with Him after we die. It also says that we have a newness of life now. In Him we can do things which are not possible for us to do alone.

Peter tells us in our text that we are to show the good works we can do. We are not just to talk about doing good or maybe even argue about it. You didn't think that iron would float in water when I told you. You had to see it. Many will not believe that you have a new power because Jesus rose from the dead. You will have to show them. When you saw iron float, you also saw the bobber. And when others see you do the works of a Christian, they will also see Christ. Amen.

The Gifts Someone Else Chose

The Word

Every good endowment and every perfect gift is from above, coming down from the Father of lights with whom there is no variation or shadow due to change. James 1:17 (From the Epistle for the Fourth Sunday After Easter)

The World

A large gift catalog

Do you like to look through gift catalogs? Most boys and girls do — and many grown people too. Look at this catalog. See, it has many gifts listed in it. It is fun just to look through the pages and to pick out the gifts you would like.

Some children like to play a game with a gift catalog. Open a page at random, like this. Then you get to pick any gift on that page. A group of children can take turns opening the catalog and seeing what kind of gifts they can choose. But that is only a game. You really don't receive the gifts you pick out. A gift catalog isn't meant for you to select gifts for yourself. A gift is something which is given to you. It is picked out by the person who gives the gift. If you use a gift catalog, you are to use it to select gifts for others, not for yourself.

Some people regard the Bible as a gift catalog. The Bible does tell us about many wonderful gifts. You could go through the Bible and read about these gifts and pick out some that you would like to have. But in our Bible reading

James tells us that these are not gifts that we can choose, but they are gifts that have already been given. We do not pick out the gifts God will give us, but He has chosen the gifts. When we read about the gifts in the Bible, we can know that these are gifts God has given to us.

First of all James mentions endowments. Endowments are gifts that cannot be seen but are a part of you; for example, your intellect, your health, your personality. We have some bad endowments, such as our greed, our prejudices, our fears. These are not from God. God gives us good endowments. One of your good endowments is your baptism. In your baptism God endowed you with the new life Christ offers to all people. The Holy Spirit has endowed you with a continuing and growing faith in Christ. Love for God is also an endowment from God, because we can love Him only because He has loved us.

James also speaks of perfect gifts. You have received many gifts in life. But the perfect gifts are from God. God's gifts are perfect because they come from a perfect God and they are given to you in perfect love. We could not possibly name all of God's perfect gifts now. But James does want you to realize that you already have these gifts and that God has chosen them for you. You have your life, created by your Father in heaven and made perfect again by Christ, who removed the guilt after you had sinned. You have the gift of the church, where you can continue to receive the message of Christ and through which you can serve Him. You have many gifts that are used in your daily life — money, possessions, friends. These, too, are perfect gifts from God when you use them as a child of God.

Look through the Bible and see other gifts from God. But don't look with the intention of picking out the ones you want. Rather read it to see the gifts God has already picked out and given to you. Amen.

Words That Work

The Word

But be doers of the Word, and not hearers only, deceiving yourselves.
James 1:22 (From the Epistle for the Fifth Sunday After Easter)

The World

A piece of typing paper about two by six inches

Do you think I can talk to this piece of paper? Of course, I can talk to it. I can talk to anything. But will it do any good? Can the paper listen to what I say? It's hard to tell if a piece of paper is listening to what you say, but let's try it.

Burn up! [*Hold the paper directly in front of mouth.*] I guess the paper wasn't listening. Or else it won't do what I said.

Let's try again. [*To paper*] Turn purple! It didn't turn purple. But I want to try once more.

Move! [*Speak forcefully so that the air from the "o" sound causes the paper to move.*] Did you see that? The paper moved when I told it to. Watch. I'll do it again.

Of course, you know why the paper moved. When you say "move," air is forced out of your mouth. The air caused the paper to move. The spoken word "move" had the power to make the paper move.

God's Word also has power to make things happen. Remember when God created the world He just said words. He said, "Let there be light," and there was light. God's words are to us like the word "move" was to the piece of paper. They have the power to make things happen.

That is why James tells us: "But be doers of the Word, and not hearers only, deceiving yourselves." Notice that it didn't tell you not to hear the Word. You are supposed to hear the Word of God, but don't stop when you've heard it. Also do it.

Sometimes we fail to do the words we heard from God because we do not understand the power they have. It is not a power to scare us into obeying Him. When we hear His law, we know that we cannot do it all. His law does not give us the power to do everything that we should. It is not enough to know what we should do. We need to find a way to do it.

The Holy Spirit gives us this way in the Gospel of Christ. When Jesus invites us to believe, He also gives us something to believe. He tells us that He has obeyed the Law for us and has died to pay for our sins. When He tells us to have hope, He gives us something to hope for. He tells us how He rose from the dead and promises that we will rise also. When Jesus tells us to love, He also gives us His love so that we can love others.

Each time you hear the Gospel of Christ, remember that the Holy Spirit works through that message. Your hearing becomes doing when you know that Christ has done all of those things for you and now continues to do them through you. Amen.

Do You Know What to Do with a Lot?

The Word

As each has received a gift, employ it for one another, as good stewards of God's varied grace. 1 Peter 4:10 (From the Epistle for the Sunday After Ascension)

The World

A large sack of candy

Would you know what to do with a piece of candy if I gave you one? I imagine you'd eat it. It doesn't take much thinking to figure out what to do with a piece of candy. Even a small baby would eat it. But would you know what to do if I gave you this whole sack of candy? You could try to eat all of it, but that might make you sick. You could keep it and eat one piece at a time. Since it was given to you, however, don't you think it would be best to share it? One piece of candy is to be eaten, but a sack of candy is to be passed around to others.

Now let's apply the same idea to another gift — the gift of God's love to you. What do you do with the love God has given to you through Christ? You can't see love like a piece of candy. But it is no less real. Jesus died on the cross to bring this love to you. Like any other gift given to you, you are to use it. Use God's love by enjoying it. Use God's love by loving God. Use God's love so you won't be lonely or afraid. Be glad that God loves you and has paid for all of your sins.

But God didn't limit the love He gave to you. He gave

you the whole sackful of love. His love to you is far beyond the amount of love which you need. It more than covers your sins. It gives you comfort greater than your sorrows. It gives you hope much greater than your fears. Now what are you going to do with that great love which Christ has given to you?

Peter suggests how you should use that love. He says, "As each has received a gift, employ it for one another, as good stewards of God's varied grace." Since you have received this gift, Peter says you should minister, that is, serve others with it. Christ has given you love beyond your own needs, but that doesn't mean it is wasted love. He tells you to pass it on to your friends.

You can give this love to others by telling them about Christ's love. You give love to others when you tell them how you are forgiven by Christ and show them that they can be forgiven too. You share love when you give comfort to others, when you spend time with the lonely, when you cheer up the sad.

It is easy to know what to do with a little love, but see if you can use the unlimited love Christ has given to you. Amen.

A Spirit That Can Be Seen

The Word

And they were all filled with the Holy Spirit. Acts 2:4a (From the Epistle for Pentecost)

The World

A small cloth sack, a ball, and a child's building block

Today is Pentecost. You heard how the Holy Spirit came to the disciples on the first Christian Pentecost. We call one Sunday a year Pentecost to remind us that the Holy Spirit comes to us also today. It is hard for us to talk about a spirit, even the Holy Spirit, because you can't see a spirit. Yet you and I can be sure that the Holy Spirit does come to us today. In one sense we can even see Him. I'll illustrate it this way:

See this sack [*sack with ball in it*]? You can see nothing but the sack, but you can tell that something is in it. Look [*twist sack tightly around the ball*]. Can you see the ball in the sack? Not really. You don't see the ball, but the ball changes the shape of the sack so that you can tell the ball is in it.

By itself the sack has no shape [*empty sack*]. It takes on the shape of whatever is in it [*place building block in the sack*]. See, the sack is now shaped like a block.

In one way you and I are like this empty sack. By ourselves we are not very much. We are weak. We can't serve God as we should. We don't live with other people as we

77

should. We need something in us to give us strength and a purpose for living.

The Holy Spirit comes to give us this strength and purpose. I can't see the Holy Spirit in you, and you can't see Him in me. I can't see a tongue of fire on your head, and I don't think you see one on mine. But we can see the Holy Spirit in each other.

We see the Holy Spirit in the same way you saw the ball in the sack. When the Holy Spirit comes into us He brings Christ into our lives. Christ in us changes the way of our lives just as the ball changed the shape of the sack. Instead of being weak, we now have the strength of Christ. Now we can live with God because Christ is God and He lives in us. Now we can live with each other because we are forgiven and can forgive each other. The Holy Spirit unites us in Christ into one family, the church.

Not only is our life not empty; it is also not filled with hate or fear or doubt. Instead we are filled with love, faith, and hope. Even though we can't see the Holy Spirit in each other, we can see the love, the faith, and the hope.

Other spirits will try to move back into our lives. Our lives are still misshapen by sin. But the Holy Spirit comes to us not only on Pentecost. He comes each time we hear of Christ's love for us. Each time He comes, He throws out the bad spirits and reshapes our lives by the life of Christ. Amen.

God in Our Language

The Word

O the depth of the riches and wisdom and knowledge of God! How unsearchable are His judgments and how inscrutable His ways! Romans 11:33 (From the Epistle for Trinity Sunday)

The World

Several children's books, a Hebrew Old Testament, and an English Bible

Most of you have read these books [*children's books*]. If you are not old enough to read, your mother or father may have read them to you. But what if you tried to read this book [*Hebrew Bible*]? Or what if someone read it to you? This book is different from the others. Not only is it larger, but you would also have to start reading it from the back. It is also written in another language, called Hebrew, which I am sure none of you can read. See — the letters and words look strange to us.

But that doesn't mean that you cannot know what this book is about. It is the Old Testament of our Bible, and it has been translated into our language [*English Bible*]. Even in English you might have a hard time understanding all of it. You have Sunday school teachers and pastors to help you understand it.

In the same way you understand these books [*children's books*], you can understand people. You can know and understand members of your family and your friends because they are like you. Just as you are a person, each of them is a person. They are happy or sad just like you. They get hungry and tired, and so do you. We can understand people because they are like us but it is difficult for us to understand God because He is not like us. Remember the words of St. Paul: "O the depth of the riches and wisdom and knowledge of God! How unsearchable are His judgments and how inscrutable His ways!" Just as we can't understand this book [*Hebrew Bible*] because it is in a different language, so we can't understand God because we are people and He is God. His knowledge and His ways are beyond us.

Yet we can know about God. God the Father sent His Son to become a human being. As the English Bible has the same message as the Hebrew Bible but presented in a way that we can understand, so also Jesus is still God but is "translated" into our way of understanding. He became a person like us. He, too, was happy or sad. He, too, became hungry and tired. Jesus did not change the message of God, but He made that message of love and mercy understandable to us because He became one of us and brought it to us.

You need a teacher to help you understand this book [*English Bible*] even if it is in your language. You also need and have a teacher to help you understand Jesus. That teacher is the Holy Spirit, who works through the message of Christ to bring us to faith and to make our faith grow.

This is why we talk about the Trinity so often in our church. It brings God to us in our language. It tells us there is God the Father, who made us all, and God the Son, who unites us with God, and the Holy Spirit, who applies the message to our lives. Amen.

A Heartful of Love

The Word

There is no fear in love, but perfect love casts out fear. 1 John 4:18a
(From the Epistle for the First Sunday After Trinity)

The World

Two water glasses, one empty, one filled with water (A small amount of ink in the water will make it visible)

What do you think is in this glass? You might think it is empty, but it is not. Even though you can't see anything, the glass is filled — filled with air. I don't have the equipment to do it here, but you can prove that a glass is filled with air. Push a glass upside down into water. No water will go up into the glass because the glass is already filled with air. So this glass is also filled with air.

Let's try to get the air out. I can't just pour the air out. It won't go out even if I shake the glass. I can't blow the air out of the glass. That might change the air, but the air is still there. Yet there is a way to get the air out. Just forget about the air and think of something else. Pour water into the glass. As the water goes in the air goes out. There is no air in the glass now because it is filled with water.

In the same way our hearts are often filled with fear. Fear is a hard subject to understand. Sometimes you may be afraid of specific things, such as a big storm or that your mother is sick or that you may get a bad grade in school. Other times you may have vague fears. You just feel that things aren't going well. Maybe you think that people don't like you. Maybe you are afraid that you won't make the grade when you grow up. Such fears may seem silly when we talk about them. But many people do have such fears.

You can't just tell fears to go away. You can't dump fear out of your heart. You certainly can't scare it out without putting another fear in. But there is one thing you can do. St. John tells you how to get rid of fear. The Bible reading says, "There is no fear in love, but perfect love casts out fear." As the water pushed air out of the glass, so love will push fear out of your heart.

This fear-chasing love is the love Christ gives to you. It is the love that has forgiven your sins, the love that promises to remain with you forever. This love is Christ's gift to you. When you have this love of Christ, you need not be afraid, for Christ is with you.

Would you like to have this love? Christ gives it to you at no cost. The Holy Spirit delivers the love of Christ to you. Do you want half a heartful? That would leave half a heart of fear. Christ offers you unlimited love. Believe in Him and receive His love. Amen.

Do as I Do

The Word

Little children, let us not love in word or speech but in deed and in truth. 1 John 3:18 (From the Epistle for the Second Sunday After Trinity)

The World

A six-year-old child

Randy, would you please come to the front to help me? Do you know how to play "Simon Says"? I'll show you. Listen to what I tell you that Simon says and do it. You may also watch my hands to see if I do what Simon says. But don't do what my hands do. Instead do what Simon says. Ready to try it?

Simon says, "Thumbs up" [*thumbs up*]. Simon says, "Thumbs down" [*thumbs down*]. Simon says, "Hold thumbs" [*wiggle thumbs*]. [*Continue at increased speed until child follows action rather than command.*] That is a hard game, isn't it, Randy? It is hard because it is easier to do what you see than what you hear. Thank you, you may return to your place.

Now I want all of you to think of another game that we sometimes play without calling it a game. It is called "Christian Says." We play the game this way:

Christian says, "Go to church." But what do Christians do? Since you are here today, you are doing what you say. Others could follow you.

Christian says, "Believe in Jesus." But what do Christians do? Do you show your faith in Jesus when you have problems? Do you show that Jesus is the most important person in your life? Do you want others to do what you do or to do what you say?

Christian says, "Love everyone." But what do Christians do? Do you always love everyone? Do you show your love to your brothers and sisters? Do you love people who are poor? Who have skin a different color than yours? Those who don't love you?

St. John tells us not to love in words or with our tongue but to love in deed and in truth. We are to love others by what we do, not by what we say. What Christian says and what he does should be the same. Remember how confusing it was when Simon said, "Thumbs up," but put his thumbs down? It is just as confusing to hear Christian say, "Love everyone," and then not show that love.

Christians often play the game wrong. But Christ shows us how to play it right. When Christ said, "Love the world" He did it. As He was nailed to the cross He didn't say, "You can go too far with this love. There's a limit to everything." Instead, He removed the limit on love by dying for our sins. You and I can learn to play "Christian Says" the right way by doing what we say. We learn what to say from Christ. Let us also learn what to do from Him. Amen.

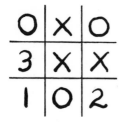

Know Your Enemy

The Word

Be sober, be watchful. Your adversary the devil prowls around like a roaring lion, seeking someone to devour. Resist him, firm in your faith. 1 Peter 5:8-9a (From the Epistle for the Third Sunday After Trinity)

The World

Tick-tack-toe game already started as illustrated (Numbers are future moves as mentioned in the sermon)

Would you like to watch this tick-tack-toe game? I am the player with "O." It is my turn. I think I see an easy way to win. I'll mark here [*No. 1*]. Then I'm sure to win, because the next time I can mark either here [*No. 2*] or here [*No. 3*]. I've got this game in the bag. But look what happens! My opponent makes his mark here [*No. 3*] and wins the game. I was so concerned about how I would win that I forgot to think about how my opponent would play.

In the same way people lose their Christian life because they do not take the time to think about what their opponent is doing to make them lose. Peter tells us: "Be sober, be watchful. Your adversary the devil prowls around like a roaring lion, seeking someone to devour. Resist him, firm in your faith." Adversary means your opponent, or your enemy. We are to be aware of our enemy, Satan.

The main message of the Bible is to tell us to know our Friend, Christ. He is our Savior and gives us a victory. But as we think about that victory, we must not forget that there is also the devil, our enemy who wants to get the best of us. We don't believe in the devil in the sense that we trust him. But we know him. We know that he does not have as much power as God and that Christ has destroyed his power over us by dying for us.

But we also know that the devil has not given up on us. If he can make us forget Christ, he can again have power over us. Therefore, we should know how he plans to defeat us. He doesn't come to us as our enemy to invite us to hell. He pretends to be a friend who gives us excuses for not following Christ. He offers us ideas and pleasures which make us forget Christ. But all the time Satan is trying to destroy us.

Therefore we should follow Peter's warning to beware of Satan. Remember that Christ has given you the victory. He came to you in Baptism to destroy the power of Satan over you. The Holy Spirit renews this victory of Christ for you each time you hear of Christ's love for you. But also remember that Satan would like to take that victory away from you. He has no power to take it away — not as long as you are with Christ. So stay with Him. Amen.

Is the Suffering Worth It?

The Word

I consider that the sufferings of this present time are not worth comparing with the glory that is to be revealed to us. Romans 8:18 (From the Epistle for the Fourth Sunday After Trinity)

The World

An eight-year-old child, a quarter, a pair of pliers, and a match

We are going to conduct an experiment. I'll hold this quarter with a pair of pliers, then use a match to make the quarter hot. Mark, will you please come here? I'll give you the quarter, Mark, if you'll take it out of the pliers. You may touch it carefully at first to see if it will burn you. Remember the quarter is yours to keep if you take it. There, that wasn't so bad, was it? You have the quarter. You may go back to your seat now.

Mark was willing to touch a hot quarter to have it. Remember that as you listen to these words: "I consider that the sufferings of this present time are not worth comparing with the glory that is to be revealed to us." It says you shouldn't complain about the troubles you now have. Instead you should think about the great joy you will have in heaven with God. Mark was willing to have two hot fingers in order to get the quarter. The thought of spending the quarter made him forget the heat. We can also put up with many problems when we remember what God has promised us.

It may not be easy to forget our troubles. Do you gripe

when you don't get your way? Do you moan and complain because you have to do some work or because you can't have something you want? If you do gripe and complain, do you realize that you are complaining against God? You are saying that He doesn't take care of you as well as you would like.

Such complaints are wrong because God has taken care of you. He has sent His Son to be your Savior. He has promised you everlasting life through Christ and will keep His promise. Before you complain, remember what God has given you and will give you.

Also remember that the problems you have can serve a good purpose. They remind you that you need Christ. Each time you feel like complaining, pray instead. Ask God to help you out of your problem and thank Him that He has removed the greatest problem of all — that is the punishment for your sins.

Don't think that you can earn heaven by putting up with the problems of this life. Mark didn't earn that quarter by taking it when it was hot. He just showed that he wanted it. I gave it to him. Christ has earned your eternal life for you by paying for your sin. When you endure the problems of this life, you just show that you want eternal life. So don't complain about everything. Instead, rejoice that you have everything. Amen.

Do You Know How to Make a Trade?

The Word

Do not return evil for evil or reviling for reviling; but on the contrary bless, for to this you have been called, that you may obtain a blessing. 1 Peter 3:9 (From the Epistle for the Fifth Sunday After Trinity)

The World

A broken balloon and a new balloon

Suppose someone asked me what I would give him for this broken balloon. [*Show that balloon is broken by blowing into it.*] A broken balloon isn't worth much; so you might wonder what I would offer for it. I know. I'll trade this new balloon for the broken one. See? [*Blow up the new balloon partway.*] This is a good one. I'll trade it for the bad one.

That might sound as if I don't know how to make a good trade. St. Peter says I made the right kind of swap. Listen to what the Bible reading says: "Do not return evil for evil or reviling for reviling; but on the contrary bless, for to this you have been called, that you may obtain a blessing." It says we shouldn't give evil for evil. That means if someone hits you, you shouldn't hit him back. If someone breaks one of your toys, you should not break his. It also says not to return reviling for reviling. Reviling means an insult. If someone says something bad about you, you are not to say anything bad about that person. It seems like a fair trade to return evil for evil, or insult for insult. But Peter says it is a bad trade.

His idea of a good trade is to give good for evil. The

other guy hits you, and you lend him your bike. The other guy says you are a "fink," and you say he is a good ball player. Sounds like a bad trade, like swapping a broken balloon for a good one. But actually it is a good trade for two reasons.

First, if you return evil for evil, then you are just as bad as the person who did the evil thing to you. He may have started it, but you are just as bad because you continued it.

But there is another, more important reason to return good for evil. The text says that you have been called to inherit a blessing. That blessing is the forgiveness of sins, which Christ has given to you. When you believe in Him, you have that blessing. You are called to receive forgiveness and to use forgiveness. You receive forgiveness when you believe in Him. You use forgiveness when you forgive the sins of others. You can give forgiveness to others who have done bad things to you because Christ has given you forgiveness. You are not losing anything when you give good for evil. You are only passing on the gift of Christ. Try it and see. It's a good swap. Amen.

The Value of Death

Do you not know that all of us who have been baptized into Christ Jesus were baptized into His death? We were buried therefore with Him by baptism into death, so that as Christ was raised from the dead by the glory of the Father, we too might walk in newness of life. Romans 6:3-4 (From the Epistle for the Sixth Sunday After Trinity)

The World

A hard-boiled egg

An egg is a rather delicate object. You know how easy it is to break one. And what good is a broken egg? Think how good this egg is. Would you like it fried, or scrambled, or maybe in a cake? [*Drop the egg*]. Don't worry. I dropped the egg on purpose. It's broken now, but it was hard-boiled; so there is no mess. The point is that the egg isn't ruined because it broke. In fact, what good is an egg that is not broken? You can't eat an egg in the shell. An egg has to be broken before you can use it. [*Take the shell off the egg.*] Now I can quit trying to protect the egg and start using it. Now it is worth something.

In the same way some people look at death as bad. Often death is spoken of as the end of everything. To some people death ruins a whole life. But it shouldn't be so. To die is like breaking the egg. We can have our full life with God only after death. Only at death are the results of sin taken away completely. Life before death is complicated by sin and sorrow and above all the fear of death. Life after death no longer fears death because it has already happened. Life after death no longer feels sin because the sting of sin, death, is gone.

All of this may sound as if you should look forward to death. That is not quite correct. Instead, you should look back to death. If you are baptized, you have already died. St. Paul says: "Do you not know that all of us who have been baptized into Christ Jesus were baptized into His death? We were buried therefore with Him by baptism into death, so that as Christ was raised from the dead by the glory of the Father, we too might walk in newness of life." You don't have to spend all your life worrying about death. Many people ruin their whole life by being afraid to die. But Christ has already died for you. He has taken the sting from death; He has paid the wages of sin — not for Himself but for you and me.

Now we can enjoy life; Christ has risen from the dead. He gave us a new life. Now we can live it, not in fear but in faith. Leaving this earth is not a threat. It is only the final step to the fulfillment of our being with Christ. The first step was made when Christ died for us. Now we can continue along the way. Amen.

The Right Kind of Freedom

When you were slaves of sin, you were free in regard to righteousness. Romans 6:20 (From the Epistle for the Seventh Sunday After Trinity)

The World

A marking pencil and a paper with the following written on it: TRUK, GLASE, STAIT, CITIE, HOOSE

A teacher gave a spelling test and asked the students to spell the following words: truck, glass, state, city, and house. One boy handed in a paper that looked like this. [*Hold up the paper.*] The boy was worried about his grade. He wasn't too sure about some of those words. He was surprised when he saw the teacher put "100%" on his paper. [*Write "100%" on paper*] But then she added another word after the 100%. She wrote "wrong." [*Add "wrong."*] Then the boy understood. He was 100% wrong. He had misspelled every word. That kind of 100% was nothing to brag about.

St. Paul talks about freedom in the same way. Freedom is good. All people should be free. But the kind of freedom the text mentions is like getting 100% wrong. It is a bad kind of freedom because it is freedom from righteousness.

Paul explains it this way. He says that sinners are slaves to their sin. They are bound by their own greed, anger, and other sinful desires. But if you are a slave to sin you are free from righteousness. Those who are willing to live in sin don't have to have a guilty conscience. They don't have to apologize to others. They don't have to confess to God. They don't have to feel sorry for others. A slave to sin is free from all those things.

But do you want that kind of freedom? A child who has no parents is also free from obeying his parents. But I am sure all orphans would like to have parents to obey. To be free from righteousness is to be free from God. But that doesn't mean that you are free. You are still bound, only you are bound to sin — bound to sin that causes sorrow and pain now and forever.

But we don't have to be slaves to sin. Christ freed the slaves by paying for our sins. Now we are slaves to righteousness. We are bound to the righteousness of Christ. Only by the good life which He lived are we free from our sin; because His good deeds paid for our bad ones. We are slaves to His righteousness because we need it every day, because we do have guilty consciences when we disobey Him, because we do want to say we are sorry, because we do feel sorry for others. But this is the kind of slavery that makes us free to live. It is 100% right. Amen.

A Member of the Team

The Word

And if children, then heirs, heirs of God and fellow heirs with Christ, provided we suffer with Him in order that we may also be glorified with Him. Romans 8:17 (From the Epistle for the Eighth Sunday After Trinity)

The World

A dart board with four darts

We are going to have a dart game. [*Hold up dart board.*] The rules are: Two men on a team. Each player throws two darts. The highest two scores are counted.

Player "A" throws first. He hits the very edge of the board. [*Place dart at edge.*] Player "B" hits the bull's-eye. Player "A" misses the board. Player "B" hits another bull's-eye. Only the two best scores are counted; so that gives their team 200 points. Of course, the other team can't beat that. Each time the first team plays the same thing happens. Player "A" either misses the board or hits the edge. But player "B" always hits the bull's-eye. So their team always wins. Both "A" and "B" get awards for being good dart players. Think what would happen if player "A" decided to play without his partner. He would lose every game. But with his partner he wins every time. His partner does the winning, but since "A" is on the team, he shares in the victory.

In the same way we are on a team with Christ. St. Paul says we are joint heirs with Christ. That means we will inherit

95

everything that He inherits. Our lives are counted together as though we were on the same team. Christ is holy, the Son of God. This holiness is counted for the team rather than just for Christ. We are sinners. We have no holiness points at all. Instead we have a balance of negative points called guilt. But our team member, Christ, died to pay for our guilt; therefore there is no negative score left. The only score is His score of holiness. We win because we are on the team.

If you or I tried to live by our own score, we could never win eternal life. But Christ has invited us to be on His team. We are on the team when we trust Him for the victory. Amen.

Learning from Others

The Word

Now these things happened to them as a warning, but they were written down for our instruction. 1 Corinthians 10:11a (From the Epistle for the Ninth Sunday After Trinity)

The World

A metal pan with no handles and two hot-pad holders

If this pan were sitting on the stove in your kitchen and the burner under it were on, it would be hot. Let's pretend that it is. Your mother calls to you and says, "Find the hot-pad holders and take the pan off the stove." You look around for the hot pads but as usual someone didn't put them back where they belong. Maybe you won't need them. You know your mother is overly careful. So you try to pick up the pan. [*Pick up pan and "react" to heat.*]

You burned your fingers. If you would have looked for the pads, and here they are, you could have done the job without being hurt. Your mother was careful because she may have gotten her fingers burned before and she wanted to warn you not to make the same mistake. But you had to learn your own way.

In the same way the Bible has many warnings for us. This is one such warning: "Now these things happened to them as a warning, but they were written down for our instruction." The Bible has many examples written for our good. It tells us about the mistakes that others have made so we do not have to make the same mistakes.

Unfortunately, however, we don't often learn by the mistakes of others. It seems that each of us must get his own fingers burned. We say, "Experience is the best teacher." But remember that experience is also the most expensive teacher. If you have to experience every mistake yourself, you are headed for trouble. But if you can see the mistakes that others have made and avoid them, you can learn the less expensive way.

For example, Moses tells us how the children of Israel didn't trust God; so they had to wander in the wilderness for 40 years. We can see then that our lack of trust often takes away the very things we want. You can learn from David's sin of lust and his efforts to hide his sin, from Thomas' doubts, from Peter's denial, from the Pharisees' pride. In all of these stories you can learn to avoid the mistakes that others have made.

But the Scripture is also filled with good examples. David repented and was forgiven. Peter wept bitter tears and received forgiveness from Christ. Thomas saw the risen Christ and said, "My Lord and my God." The publican teaches us humility.

The bad examples are the hot pan. Avoid them. The good examples are the hot-pad holders. Look for them and use them. Amen.

The Way We Can Think Alike

The Word

Therefore I want you to understand that no one speaking by the Spirit of God ever says "Jesus be cursed!" and no one can say "Jesus is Lord" except by the Holy Spirit. 1 Corinthians 12:3 (From the Epistle for the Tenth Sunday After Trinity)

The World

The church hymnal (Any other reading material available to all the listeners may be substituted. Select a short, easily found section to be read together.)

Please open your hymnal to the first page. It has a number of prayers. The first one is "A Prayer upon Entering Church." All of you who can read, please join in praying this prayer as we read it aloud.

Do you think it was strange that we could all say the same words without practicing? Of course not, because we were all reading from the same book. Since the books were the same, our words also were the same.

On the other hand, if someone read different words than the rest of us, we would know that his book was different. If we all had different books, we could not read together. Some would be saying one thing, while others said something else.

Paul tells us that we can all speak about Jesus in the same way because we have the same Spirit. Anyone who speaks about Jesus in a different way does not have that same Spirit. Remember the part which said: "Therefore I want you to understand that no one speaking by the Spirit of God ever says 'Jesus be cursed' and no one can say 'Jesus is Lord' except by the Holy Spirit."

Think of how many people believe in Christ. But each person did not make up his own faith. The Holy Spirit has brought the message of Christ to each of us. When we all read from the same book, we could say the same words. When the same Spirit guides us, we can all know the same Savior, who has forgiven our sins.

However, if anyone speaks against Christ, he is not guided by the Holy Spirit. If two people read from different books, they won't say the same words. So also if we deny things about Christ which the Spirit tells us, then we are not listening to the Holy Spirit.

If we want to be guided by God's Spirit, we cannot make up our own ideas about our faith. Instead, we go to the power the Holy Spirit uses to guide us — the Scriptures. Then we are all guided by the same Spirit to worship the same Savior. Amen.

You Can't Give What You Don't Have

The Word

For I delivered to you as of first importance what I also received, that Christ died for our sins in accordance with the Scriptures, that He was buried, that He was raised on the third day in accordance with the Scriptures. 1 Corinthians 15:3-4 (From the Epistle for the Eleventh Sunday After Trinity)

The World

An apple

Pretend that I am hungry right now. You know that I am not, but since we are pretending, pretend that I am about to die of hunger. What would you do about it? I hope you would give me something to eat, but do you have any food with you? You can't give me money because I can't buy food here. The food you have at home doesn't do me any good here. I don't think that you have any food with you in church. A piece of bubble gum wouldn't be of much help to me.

But what if your mother gave you this? [*Show the apple*.] Then you would have something to give me. An apple would be the right food for a hungry person. But you couldn't give me the apple until someone gave it to you. You can't give what you don't have.

In the same way Paul tells us that he gave the same message to the people that was given to him. He says: "For I delivered to you as of first importance what I also received, that

Christ died for our sins in accordance with the Scriptures, that He was buried, that He was raised on the third day in accordance with the Scriptures." Paul didn't have his own idea on how to help the Corinthian people. But Paul knew what had been given to him that was of great help to him. He had been told about the death of Jesus. Someone had explained to him that Jesus had died for his sins. Paul had found out about Christ's resurrection from the dead. He knew that because Christ lived he would live also. Since Paul had received this help from knowing Jesus, he told the people in Corinth about the same help.

So also if you want to help others by giving them the Gospel, you must first receive it. It is not selfish for you to think that you have to receive the Gospel first. Unless you have it, you can't give it to anyone else. You are receiving that Gospel now in church. You also receive it in Sunday school and vacation Bible school. You receive it when you read your Bible. Some of you will soon be in confirmation classes, where you will also receive the Gospel.

Because you are receiving it, you can also give it to others. If your friends had no food, you would divide your food with them. All of your friends need the forgiveness which Christ offers. Will you share it with them? Amen.

Your Spiritual Life Preserver

The Word

Such is the confidence that we have through Christ toward God. Not that we are sufficient of ourselves to claim anything as coming from us; our sufficiency is from God. 2 Corinthians 3:4-5 (From the Epistle for the Twelfth Sunday After Trinity)

The World

A child's life preserver

Tommy went on a vacation with his parents to a cabin at a big lake. Tommy didn't know how to swim. Every day he begged to go into the deep lake. His parents finally gave him one of these [*life preserver*]. They put it around Tommy's body and strapped it on tight. You know what happened when Tommy jumped into the water. He floated on top. It was easy and fun. He wanted to go back again and again. Each time his mother would carefully put on the life preserver for him.

One time Tommy wanted to go swimming when his mother wasn't around. To him it seemed simple to play on top of the water. He forgot all about the life preserver. "I can swim by myself," he thought as he ran to the lake and jumped in. Without the preserver he sank in the water and almost drowned before someone pulled him out.

In the same way God has sent His Son to be our life preserver. God has told us that if we are to live with Him now or forever, we must obey His commandments. To swim you have to stay on top of the water. To live with God you have to stay on top of the Law. But we can't obey all the commandments. We are sinners. Every day we sink to the bottom. But Christ has come to obey the Law for us. He is our life preserver who holds us up. Through Him all our sins are forgiven, and we can live with God now and forever. St. Paul calls that our trust in God through Christ.

Our Bible reading also says that our sufficiency is not of ourselves, but our sufficiency is of God. That means we must not think it is because we are good that we are forgiven. It is not to our credit that we will live with God now and forever. Without Christ, our Life Preserver, we would sink to the bottom. We depend entirely on Him.

Little Tommy may learn how to swim, so he won't need the life preserver. But we cannot be holy by ourselves. We will always need Jesus to hold us up. And we have Him because He came to us. Amen.

It Can't Be Fixed

The Word

But the Scripture consigned all things to sin, that what was promised to faith in Jesus Christ might be given to those who believe. Galatians 3:22 (From the Epistle for the Thirteenth Sunday After Trinity)

The World

Two children's magazines, exactly alike (Sunday school booklets could be used), and a roll of tape

This is an interesting magazine about boys and girls. I think some of you would enjoy reading it. Oops! [*Tear a page.*] I'm sorry that I tore it. But I think it can be fixed. [*Use tape to repair the tear.*] There it is as good as new, well almost as good as new. This page is just an advertisement. I'll tear it out and throw it away. [*Tear out page and wad it up.*] Oh, I shouldn't have done that. The back of that page had something important on it. Do you think I could put this page back in? [*Try to straighten out page.*] Now another page is loose; because I tore this one out. [*Remove other pages.*] This whole magazine is falling apart. [*Pull out other pages.*] This magazine can't be repaired. I might as well admit that I ruined this magazine and throw it away. Then I can get a new one and have a good magazine. [*Show the other magazine.*] This one is in good shape.

In the same way our lives have been destroyed by sin. Sometimes we think we can patch up our own lives by doing something good every time we do something wrong. But the scar of the sin is still there. We can try to ignore sin, but that doesn't make it go away. When we look at our lives, we know St. Paul is right when he says that everyone is under sin. We are sinners. Our lives have been destroyed like the magazine.

But the purpose of knowing that we are sinners is not just to make us give up and throw our lives away. Paul says he wants you to know that you are a sinner so you can receive the promise of faith which Christ gives to all who believe. The promise is that you have a new life. Jesus has lived for you. He has replaced your sinful life with His holy life. He wants you to see that you can't fix up your own life. Only when you see that your own life has been destroyed by sin, can you reach for the new life that Christ offers to you.

When you think of your sin, see it as this magazine, which is destroyed so that it can't be repaired. But also think of the new magazine that replaced it. It is the new life that Christ offers you. Amen.

Stop-and-Go Religion

The Word

Now the works of the flesh are plain: immorality, . . . strife, jealousy, anger, selfishness, dissension, party spirit, envy, drunkenness, carousing, and the like. I warn you, as I warned you before, that those who do such things shall not inherit the kingdom of God. But the fruit of the Spirit is love, joy, peace, patience, kindness, goodness, faithfulness, gentleness, self-control; against such there is no law. Galatians 5:19-24 (From the Epistle for the Fourteenth Sunday After Trinity)

The World

A stoplight drawn on heavy paper (Hinge a card in the middle of the picture with "Stop" on one side and "Go" on the other. Light may be changed from "Go" to "Stop" by flipping the card.)

You recognize this [*sign with "Stop" showing*]. It is a stoplight. It tells car drivers to stop. There are other kinds of stoplights. Boys and girls are told to stop often. Stop fighting. Stop playing with your food. Stop crying. You are used to stop signs.

The Bible also has many stop signs. St. Paul gave us a long list of stop signs in today's Bible reading. He tells you to stop immorality, stop strife, stop being jealous, stop getting angry, stop being selfish. There are even more stop signs in this long list of things which we are not to do. Paul not only tells us not to do such things but he tells us why. These things are against the will of God. God has put up the stop sign. When you are tempted to do those things, you should remember the stop sign God has put before such acts.

But our religion is not a "Stop" religion. The purpose of Christianity is not to tell you what not to do. It tells you what Christ has done for you. It tells you what you can do through Him. We get the wrong view of Christianity if we think only about the "Stop" part. Like this light. We call it a "Stop" light. But it is also a "Go" light. [*Flip to "Go."*] The light does not just tell us to stop. It also tells us to go. God only tells us to stop when we are going in the wrong direction. He then shows us the right direction to go.

St. Paul also tells you about the "Go" light. Listen: "The fruit of the Spirit is love, joy, peace, patience, kindness, goodness faithfulness, gentleness, self-control; against such there is no law." These are "Go" signs. These are things you can do because you have the power of Christ. Without Him, your religion would be only a "Stop" religion. [*Flip to "Stop."*] But through His grace you have the power to serve God. His "Go" sign is an invitation to use the new life He gives to you.

You still need the stoplight. You need it to see your sin. You need to see that through faith in Christ your sins are forgiven. Then the light changes to "Go" [*flip to "Go"*] as you serve Christ out of love for Him. Amen.

Are You Spending or Saving Life?

The Word

Do not be deceived; God is not mocked, for whatever a man sows, that he will also reap. For he who sows to his own flesh will from the flesh reap corruption; but he who sows to the Spirit will from the Spirit reap eternal life. Galatians 6:7-8 (From the Epistle for the Fifteenth Sunday After Trinity)

The World

A piggy bank, two dimes, and a nickel

It is time to get your weekly allowance. Here it is: two dimes and a nickel. You have this piggy bank. It is empty. [*Shake bank.*] You decide it would be nice to save some money in the bank and spend some. If you put a dime into the bank, you could save up for something special. But this week you want to buy some things, so you spend all 25 cents. Next week you get two dimes and a nickel again. Again you spend it all. This happens week after week. Nothing goes into the piggy bank.

One day you see a special toy you want. It costs 69 cents. But your allowance is only 25 cents. So you go home to open your piggy bank to get the rest of the money. But the bank is empty. You didn't put anything into it, so you can't take anything out of it.

St. Paul says the same thing. "Whatever a man sows, that he will also reap!" That means whatever you work for is what you will receive. If you had saved the money in the bank, you would have had money for the special toy. Since you had already spent the money, nothing was left. It is bad to be without money when you need it, but it is much worse to be without God when you need Him. The same idea of sowing and reaping applies to your life with God. Are you spending your life, or is God saving it? Think about what God means to you now.

Do you want to be with God? Answer by what you do with your life, rather than what you say. If you do not read God's Word, if you don't go to His house, if you don't ask Him for help, if you don't thank Him for what He has given you, if you don't want to follow His commands — if you do not do these things, how can you say you want to be with God? You are spending your life on yourself. If you don't want to be with God now, what makes you think you'll want to be with Him forever?

But you can be with God now. As you read His Word, you learn that Christ has forgiven your sins. When you come to church, you worship Him, you ask for His help, and you thank Him for His blessings. As you learn more about Christ, you see how He helps you in your daily life. Instead of spending your life on yourself, you find that Christ has saved it for you. Then you are with Him now and forever. "He who sows to the Spirit will from the Spirit reap eternal life." Amen.

Rooted in the Love of Christ

The Word

Christ will live in your hearts by faith, and you will be firmly rooted and built up in love so that you and all the holy people can grasp how broad and long and high and deep love is, and know how Christ loves us — more than we can know — and so you will be filled with all that is in God. Ephesians 3:17-19 (From the Epistle for the Sixteenth Sunday After Trinity [Beck])

The World

A short piece of clothes line, a dollar bill, and a large cross

St. Paul tells us that we are to have roots. Let's pretend that this rope is our root. See, it is strong. It could hold us firm and solid as roots hold a tree firmly in place. One end of the root is fastened to me. [*Tie an end of the rope around wrist.*] But for me to be rooted, the other end of the rope must be fastened to something. If one end of the rope is fastened to me and the other end dangling, I would be like a tree that had been uprooted.

We place our roots in whatever we trust. Suppose I trusted in money. [*Tie dollar bill to the other end of the rope.*] The root can be strong, but it is no stronger than whatever it is rooted in. I wouldn't want my life to depend on the strength of money. Money cannot give health or happiness. It certainly cannot give us eternal life.

Some people trust in themselves. [*Tie the end of the rope to the other wrist.*] But if I trust in my own strength or

111

knowledge, if I depend on myself, I really have no roots at all, because the root is fastened only to me. I have no way to get any strength except from myself.

St. Paul says we are to be rooted in the love of Christ by our faith in Him. We can picture this by tying the rope to this cross. The cross shows us how Christ loves us because He died for our sins. Our faith trusts in Christ. It is like this rope that connects us to Christ. The faith is as strong as that to which it is tied. When we trust in Christ, we are rooted firmly in His love.

Being rooted in Christ helps us live now. When we are happy, we know that our joy is a gift from God. Because our roots are in Him we know that He loves us. We know that He is with us at all times. But being rooted in Christ also helps us when we are sad or have great problems. Many temptations pull us away from God, but roots in Christ hold us close to Him. Many sorrows make us wonder why God allows such things to happen. But roots in Christ gives us strength to continue in faith even in such sorrows.

Being rooted in Christ also shows us that life cannot be destroyed by death. Our roots bring us the source of life. Being rooted to the ever-living Christ means we share the everlasting life He has given to us. Amen.

A Set of People Called Christians

The Word

Be eager to maintain the unity of the Spirit in the bond of peace. There is one body and one Spirit, just as you are called to the one hope that belongs to your call, one Lord, one faith, one baptism, one God and Father of us all, who is above all and through all and in all. Ephesians 4:3-6 (From the Epistle for the Seventeenth Sunday After Trinity)

The World

A set of checkers (one color only) and the following pieces from a Monopoly set: piece of money, title to property, die, house, and a player's marker

Most of you know how to play checkers. This is a set of checkers. We call these pieces a set because they belong together. You can tell that they belong together because they are all the same size, the same shape, and they all serve the same purpose. It makes no difference where you put these pieces on the checkerboard. They are all alike.

Sometimes we Christians feel that we are to be like this set of checkers. In a way we are a set. Christians belong together. God has called us away from sin to be together with Him and with each other. But sometimes it is difficult for us Christians to feel like a set. We don't seem to belong together. You can't look at us and see that we belong together as you can see that these checkers are a set. We are not all the same color. We don't speak the same language. We can't all do the same things. We often feel alone because we don't see how we belong to other Christians and how they belong to us.

But we Christians are a set of people. We do belong together. To see how we belong together, let's look at another game which you may have played. [*Hold up various pieces of Monopoly — one at a time.*] See these pieces. They don't look alike. They are not made of the same material — some are paper, some wood, others plastic. They are different colors and shapes. They do not serve the same purpose. Yet they are a set because they belong together and work together. If you have ever played Monopoly, you recognize all of these pieces as parts of a Monopoly set. If you don't know the game, these pieces all seem alone. They have nothing in common. But if you know the game, you know that these pieces belong together.

In the same way we Christians are a set of people who belong together — not because we look alike, not because we all serve the same purpose. The one thing that makes us belong together is that we all have the same Savior. St. Paul says that we are all one body. All people who believe in Christ belong together just as all of these pieces belong to the same game. We are all one because we have one Spirit, one Lord, one faith, one baptism, one God and Father of us all. The same Holy Spirit comes to all Christians and leads us to the same Savior, Jesus Christ. We all have one faith because we believe in this same Savior. "One baptism" does not mean that we were all baptized once for all time; it means that all who are baptized into Christ have that one baptism which Christ Himself has given.

Let us remember the union we have in Christ. Remember that we Christians are a set of people who work together because we are united in Christ. You and I can do this when we let others see our faith in Christ and when we look for that faith in others. Amen.

114

God's Offer to Make You Rich

The Word

In every way you were enriched in Him with all speech and all knowledge — even as the testimony to Christ was confirmed among you — so that you are not lacking in any spiritual gift, as you wait for the revealing of our Lord Jesus Christ. 1 Corinthians 1:5-7 (From the Epistle for the Eighteenth Sunday After Trinity)

The World

A dollar bill, a savings account book, several items of jewelry

God wants to make you rich. Will you let Him? I am sure that all of you would like to be rich. But how do you want to be rich? To be rich means to have a lot of something, to be well supplied. Often we think that being rich means to have lots of money. [*Show dollar bill.*] None of you would think that you were rich if you had only one dollar like this. But if you had this building full of dollar bills, you would be rich — rich in money, that is.

But do you know that you can be rich without having any money? Most people don't keep very much money. They put it in the bank. [*Show bank book.*] You might not have any money in your pocket, but if you had a big bank balance, you would still be rich in money. Or you might not even have any money in the bank and still be rich. [*Show jewelry.*] Of course, these are not real diamonds and gold, but if they were, and you owned them, you would be rich — rich in jewelry. Some person might not have any money, but he might own a lot of land. He would be rich — rich in land.

There are other ways to be rich. In our Bible reading Paul tells you that God wants to make you rich in your speech and knowledge. I cannot show you that kind of riches in my hands, like money and jewelry. Yet that kind of riches can be seen because it changes our lives. That's why God wants to make you rich. He wants you to be rich in what you know about Him and what you say because in these riches you receive not only the gifts of God but also God Himself.

Paul also tells you how God offers to make you rich. He says that He confirms the testimony of Christ in you. That means that the Holy Spirit makes you sure of all the things that Christ did and said. God makes you rich in knowledge of Him by telling you how Christ loves you and gave His life for you. He makes you rich in your speech by giving you the joy of knowing that Christ was born for you; that even after He died He lives again so you might always live. He makes you rich in knowledge by letting you know of Christ's promise to be with you now and His promise that He has a place for you in heaven.

God offers you the greatest of all riches when He makes you rich in knowledge of Him. All of these riches (money, bankbook, and jewelry) can be lost, stolen, or destroyed. They are temporary riches. But the permanent riches are those which God gives through His Son. You can be rich in money and not have health. You can be rich in health and not be happy. But with God's gift of riches in knowledge of Christ you have all the spiritual gifts that promise the love of Christ now and forever. Amen.

You Can Tell a Christian by His Cover

The Word

Put off your old nature, which belongs to your former manner of life and is corrupt through deceitful lusts, and be renewed in the spirit of your mind, and put on the new nature, created after the likeness of God in true righteousness and holiness. Ephesians 4:22-24 (From the Epistle for the Nineteenth Sunday After Trinity)

The World

A child's book with an old, dull cover and a new, attractive cover (The first cover may be made from a grocery sack. It should be dirty, with marks of wear and tear.)

Do you like to pick your books from the library? It is difficult to tell much about a book by its cover; yet the cover does tell us something. If you saw this book [*hold up book with the old cover*] at the library, would you want to read it? It looks old and dull. I doubt that many boys and girls would check this book out. In fact, the librarian might just as well throw this book away or put it up on a high shelf out of everyone's way.

But look at the same book now. [*Remove the old cover and put on the new*.] Doesn't it look interesting to you? Many boys and girls would like to read this book. The librarian might even put it out on a special table for everyone to see. Yet this is the same book you saw before. Only the cover has been changed. It makes the entire book seem different.

In some ways we are like the book with the old cover.

117

[*Show first cover.*] Because we sin, we give a bad impression to those who see us. When we lie, when we get angry, when we say bad things, when we disobey parents, we are showing others what we really are. People can tell what we are like by our actions, just as you decide what a book is like by its cover. God also sees what we are. We may wonder why God doesn't throw us away like an old book when He sees our sin. But He doesn't. Instead, St. Paul tells us to put off our sinful nature and to put on the new nature of God. Instead of showing people our sin, we should show God's goodness.

It looks so easy to change the cover of the book, to make it new and fresh. But remember, the book didn't change itself. Neither can we. But God can change us. Christ came to pay for our guilt. He died for us because we have sinned by telling lies, by saying bad things, by hurting others. When He died for us, He took away our bad cover of evil. In its place He gives us His own cover of holiness and goodness. When we are forgiven by Christ we no longer have to show the whole world how evil we are. Instead, we can show how good God is.

When you sin against God, ask Christ to forgive you. Then think of Him taking away your sin as I remove this old cover from the book [*show it*]. Then think also of Him as He puts on this new cover [*show it*]. The new cover of your life is as good and as holy as Christ because it is Christ. You can tell a Christian by his cover because he is covered by Christ. Amen.

How Do You Spend Your Time?

The Word

Look carefully then how you walk, not as unwise but as wise, making the most of the time, because the days are evil. Therefore do not be foolish, but understand what the will of the Lord is. Ephesians 5:15-17 (From the Epistle for the Twentieth Sunday After Trinity)

The World

A dollar bill, a child's toy worth about a dollar, a toy worth about 10 cents

Our Bible reading says we should make the most of our time. Time is hard to understand because we can't see it. I could show you a clock or a calendar, but they are not time. Yet we all know that we have time. And we all have to use our time. Paul wants to help us use our time the right way; so I ask you: How do you spend your time?

Since we can't see time, I'll use this dollar. At least you can understand spending a dollar. By seeing the ways you can spend a dollar, we will also learn something about spending our time.

You could spend the dollar on a toy worth a dollar. [*Show toy.*] You have spent the dollar, but you still have the value of a dollar because the toy is worth a dollar. Or you could buy this toy [*show cheap toy*] with your dollar. It is only worth 10 cents. The dollar would be gone, and you would have only 10 cents' worth to show for it. Or you could just throw the dollar away. [*Wad up bill and throw it away*.] Then the dollar is gone, and you have nothing to show for it.

Now let's think about spending time in the same way. Sometimes we throw away our time as I threw away the dollar bill. Of course, I can again pick up the dollar I threw away. But if you throw away time, you can never get it back again. It is gone. You can also spend your time by getting only part of its value — like buying a 10-cent toy with a dollar. You and I do this when we use our time carelessly and without thinking about it. We should use our time by getting its full value — like buying a dollar toy for a dollar. When you use your time by getting its value out of it, then it is not gone. Instead, you have spent it for something worthwhile. The time will be gone, but you will have something to show for it, even if it is only a good memory.

Of course, the big question is: On what should you spend your time? Is time spent worthwhile if you earn some money, have some fun, learn something? Paul says that the wise way to spend time is to understand what the will of the Lord is. Do you understand that it is God's will that He live with you and you with Him? Do you understand that in Christ this is possible because He lives in us? Do you use your time with the awareness that Christ is with you? Time that is spent with Christ is well spent. It is well spent because you do not lose its value. Christ is with us now so we can be with Him forever. Time with Christ does not end. It lasts forever. Amen.

Put On the Whole Armor of God

The Word

Take the whole armor of God, that you may be able to withstand in
the evil day, and having done all, to stand. Stand therefore, having
girded your loins with truth, and having put on the breastplate of righteousness, and having shod your feet with the equipment of the Gospel
of peace; above all taking the shield of faith, with which you can
quench all the flaming darts of the evil one. And take the helmet of
salvation, and the sword of the Spirit, which is the Word of God. Ephesians 6:13-17 (From the Epistle for the Twenty-first Sunday After Trinity)

The World

A paper doll with the following items of clothing: coat, snowpants, winter boots, scarf, winter hat, and gloves. Signs with the following printed
in large letters: Gospel, Truth, Righteousness, Faith, Salvation, Word of
God

It won't be long until the weather will be cold. Let's get ready
for the cold weather by dressing this paper doll to play out in
the snow. The doll will need snowpants [*put on doll's items
of clothing as their names are mentioned*], a coat, a hat, a
scarf, and gloves. Now [*hold up doll*], if this doll were you,
would you be ready to go out and play in the snow? Not
quite. Look at the bare feet. It would not help to have your
hands, ears, and neck nice and warm if your feet were bare in
the snow. [*Add the boots.*] But that doesn't mean the boots
are the most important thing to wear. If you had the boots
on, but no hat or scarf [*remove them*], you couldn't play in

121

the snow either. To play outdoors you need your whole body protected from the cold, not just part of it.

In the same way, our Bible reading tells us, we need our entire life protected from the power of the devil. Paul tells us to put on the whole armor of God — not just part of it, but all of it. Then he names the parts of the armor. He tells us to put on the Gospel. [*Hold up "Gospel."*] You know that the Gospel is the Good News that Christ is our Savior. You might think that it is enough just to have the Gospel. But Paul reminds us that we have to apply this Gospel to our lives by understanding what it is. We need also the Truth. [*Hold up sign.*] We have the truth because Christ is the truth. We also need Righteousness. [*Hold up sign.*] Christ gave us His righteousness, and we are to wear it as a part of our armor. Our response to the Gospel is Faith. [*Hold up sign.*] Salvation [*hold up sign*] means that we have been rescued from sin and death. We are now saved from the power of the devil over us. Finally Paul tells us to wear the Word of God. [*Hold up sign.*] The Word of God is the Bible, which tells us the Gospel and gives us all the other parts of the armor of God. Remember that all of these things [*show signs*] are God's. They are His protection against the devil. But He has given them to us to wear so that we are protected from the power of the evil one.

If we are to fight against the devil we must use all of them. Just as the doll would not have been protected from the cold if it did not have the boots, so we are not protected from the devil unless we have the whole armor of God. God gives you this armor each time you hear the message of Christ. Put on the armor by believing the message of the Gospel and by using it to fight against the temptations of the devil. Amen.

A Job Well Done

The Word

I am sure that He who began a good work in you will bring it to completion at the day of Jesus Christ. Philippians 1:6 (From the Epistle for the Twenty-second Sunday After Trinity)

The World

A dirty dinner plate (red, yellow, and brown water colors will give the plate a used look and be less offensive than the real thing) with one half washed clean

I suppose that most of you boys and girls help your mother with the dishes. Suppose that you had helped with the dishes and you had washed this plate [*show plate*] and put it away. What would your mother say when she took the plate out to use it for the next meal? She would probably say that you hadn't washed the plate. You might say that you had washed the plate by pointing to this side, which is clean. But this clean side of the plate doesn't prove anything until the entire plate is clean. I wouldn't want to eat off of this plate, would you? The clean half wouldn't help any because a job isn't done until it is completed.

In the same way Paul in our Bible reading for today talks about God's job of saving us. First he mentions that God has begun a good work in us. The good work God has started in us is our salvation. God does not wait until the day we die to save us from hell. Those who believe in Christ are saved from hell now, because God's plan of salvation is not just to save us from hell but to save us for Himself. God has made us His children now by giving us His Son to pay for our sins.

When we hear the message of Christ our Savior, our sins are washed away. But sometimes we are afraid that we are like this plate. [*Show plate*.] Our sins are washed away now [*clean side of plate*]. But what about the rest of our life [*dirty side of plate*]? What if God would get tired of forgiving us? What if He would lose His patience with sinners like us and quit forgiving us? What if God started the job of saving us and then quit?

But Paul tells us that God will not quit. He says, "I am sure that He who began a good work in you will bring it to completion at the day of Jesus Christ." God does not quit when a job is half done. He tells us that Christ is our Savior today. He will continue to give us this assurance until the day of Jesus Christ — that is, Judgment Day, when Christ comes to take us to be with Him.

This message tells us that we need not be afraid that God will quit loving us. It also shows us why we must always trust in God to save us. If we trust in ourselves, we are afraid that we might quit loving God. Many people have left God. Adam and Eve did. Judas left Jesus. Jesus told a parable about people who believed for a while but in time of temptation fell away. Paul told some of the Galatians that they were cut off from Christ. People often do a job only half way. But God completes the work He starts. He has saved you today. He will keep you forever. Amen.

For Whom Are You Waiting?

The Word
Our commonwealth is in heaven, and from it we await a Savior, the Lord Jesus Christ. Philippians 3:20 (From the Epistle for the Twenty-third Sunday After Trinity)

The World
Several pieces of candy, a letter ready for mailing, and a dollar bill

Suppose I had knocked on your door at Halloween. If you would have opened the door and handed me several pieces of candy [*show candy*], I would have known that you weren't expecting me. You would have been expecting some boys and girls who were out trick-or-treating. In fact, I can sometimes tell whom people are expecting when I knock on their door. If someone opens the door with a letter [*show letter*] in his hand, he was probably waiting for the mailman, not me. Sometimes people open the door with money in their hands. [*Show dollar.*] They are waiting for someone to collect money — probably the paper boy.

In the same way, Jesus can tell if we are waiting for Him by seeing what we are doing. In the Bible reading Paul says, "Our commonwealth is in heaven, and from it we await a Savior, the Lord Jesus Christ." By our faith in Christ we already know we are going to heaven. It is our commonwealth, that is, our homeland. And we are waiting for Christ to come to take us home. We know that Judgment Day will be at hand at Christ's coming. We are to wait for that Day by being ready for Him to come. Just as I can tell whom people are waiting for by what they have in their hands when they open their door for me, so Christ can tell if we are waiting for Him by what we are doing.

What would you like to have Christ find you doing when He comes? You might say that you would like to be in church, or reading your Bible, or saying your prayers. Those are important things to do. But you can't wait to do them just when Christ returns. He is already with us as our Savior. You are to do those things not just to put on an act for Him but because you want to hear what He has to say now and because you want to talk to Him.

But what if Christ finds a baseball and glove in your hands when He comes back? Or finds you watching TV? Do you think that would be bad? I don't think so. As we wait for Christ, we can enjoy the life we now have. We can be eager to go to heaven and yet glad to be on this earth, for God has also made the life we now have, and Christ is with us now too. But as we enjoy the many nice things of this earth, remember two things: first, remember that we can enjoy them only because we know that Christ is our Savior and that our sins are forgiven; second, remember that we will gladly leave all of this behind to go to heaven. You can enjoy a TV program, but when Christ comes, you cannot say, "Wait until this program is over; then I'll go with You." When Christ comes, we will gladly leave everything behind.

When He comes, we should be doing His will, and that is that we live with Him. You might be in church, you might be helping your parents, you might be studying, you might be playing, you might be eating or sleeping. All of these things can be doing the will of God when you know that Christ is with you. Amen.

Rescued for a Purpose

The Word
He has delivered us from the dominion of darkness and transferred us to the kingdom of His beloved Son, in whom we have redemption, the forgiveness of sins. Colossians 1:13-14 (From the Epistle for the Twenty-fourth Sunday After Trinity)

The World
A paper sack filled with assorted waste paper, including the cardboard tube from a paper towel roll, and a piece of violet wrapping paper

Do you ever carry the trash out for your mother? This sack of waste paper is like that in many homes. [*Show sack.*] It has to be carried out to be burned or for the garbage man to pick up. If you are like many other children, you like to go through the trash and keep things. Suppose you looked into this sack and saw this tube from a paper towel roll. [*Show tube*]. You might decide to keep it. But your mother would ask you what you wanted it for. There is no use in keeping this from the trash today only to throw it away tomorrow. If you had no reason to keep the tube, your mother would probably tell you to throw it away.

But maybe you do have a use for this tube. See, if you wrapped the tube with this colored paper, it would look like a candle [*wrap it*]. It could be used for an Advent candle or for a Christmas decoration. Then you would have a purpose in keeping the tube. You could take it out of the trash and put it in a place of honor.

In the same way, God has taken us from the trash and placed us in an honored place. The Bible reading says, "He has delivered us from the dominion of darkness and transferred us to the kingdom of His beloved Son, in whom we have redemption, the forgiveness of sins."

Because of our sins we belonged to the kingdom of darkness. We were like that sack of trash ready to be thrown out because we had no purpose in life. But God saved us from being thrown out. He didn't just delay the time when we would be thrown out. He didn't just take us out of the kingdom of darkness for a while. He took us from the kingdom of darkness and put us into the kingdom of His beloved Son.

In this new kingdom we have a purpose in living. We were saved by God for a reason. The reason is that we can now serve Him in this new kingdom. Just as the paper tube was saved from the trash and made into something useful, so God has saved us from hell and made us useful. By the power of Christ we can serve God. We can worship Him. We can share His love with other people. We can speak to other people about His great gift in Christ. We can enjoy the life He has given to us. All of these things arre fulfilled in the purpose of our life. We can do this only because God has removed our guilt and has taken us from the kingdom of darkness and placed us into His kingdom.

Remember what God has done for you and enjoy your life in His kingdom by being His child now. Amen.

Comfort Where It Counts

The Word

We would not have you ignorant, brethren, concerning those who are asleep, that you may not grieve as others do who have no hope. For since we believe that Jesus died and rose again, even so, through Jesus, God will bring with Him those who have fallen asleep. . . . Therefore comfort one another with these words. 1 Thessalonians 4:13-14, 18 (From the Epistle for the Twenty-fifth Sunday After Trinity)

The World

A photograph of a person (which you are willing to destroy) and its negative

See this picture. Pictures like this are very cheap — that is, they do not cost very much. But some pictures are very valuable. Let's pretend that this is a picture of a friend who has now moved a long way from here. Even though the picture didn't cost very much, it would be valuable. It reminds me of my friend. I want to remember how he looked. I have to take good care of the picture because the friend is far away and I cannot take another picture.

Suppose this picture were destroyed. [*Tear the picture into small pieces.*] Since this picture was valuable to me, you know that I would be unhappy. How would you try to help me? Would you say that the picture wasn't very good anyway? That wouldn't help, because I thought the picture was good. Would you tell me to forget about it? Or to think about something else? Or just to remember that once I enjoyed the picture. Those statements would not help me. But there would be one way you could help me. You could make me forget all about the sadness of losing the picture. You could comfort me by reminding me that I have this. [*Show the negative.*] This is the negative of the picture that was torn up. With this negative I can forget that the picture was destroyed, for I can get the same picture back again.

In our Bible reading Paul tells us to use the same kind of comfort for each other when a loved one dies. Many people die each day. Most of them are not important to the world, but they are important to the people who love them. We are sad when someone we love dies because we miss the person and because we know that we cannot have him back.

But Paul says that we should not be ignorant about those people who have died and that we don't have to be sad. "For since we believe that Jesus died and rose again, even so, through Jesus, God will bring with Him those who have fallen asleep." Death does not destroy a person. Because Christ died for us and rose again, we know that we, too, can live after death. Just as you can't destroy a picture as long as you can have a new picture made from the negative, so also death does not destroy those who believe in Christ, because they will come back from the dead.

Paul also tells us to use these words to comfort one another. You might remember the picture and the negative as a way to tell your friends of everlasting life when someone they love has died. You can also remember this comfort for yourself as you think of your loved ones who have died. We have comfort because Christ gives it to us. Amen.

The Patience of God

The Word

The Lord is not slow about His promise as some count slowness, but is forbearing toward you, not wishing that any should perish, but that all should reach repentance. But the day of the Lord will come like a thief. 2 Peter 3:9-10a (From the Epistle for the Twenty-sixth Sunday After Trinity)

The World

Three clear plastic containers, all the same size — one filled with dried beans, one filled with eggs, and one empty

Do you know the difference between being slow and being patient? Let me see if I can show you. See this container full of beans. What if your mother told you to put all the beans into this empty container? As soon as you finish the job you are to go to bed. If you didn't want to go to bed, you could delay a long time by doing the job like this. [*Take one bean at a time from the full container and carefully place it into the empty one.*] That is being slow. Your mother would tell you to pour the beans like this. [*Pour all of them into the empty container.*] Then the job is done. Putting the beans in one at a time would be called being slow.

Suppose your mother told you to put these eggs [*show full container*] into the empty container. As soon as you are done, you get to watch TV. Now your favorite TV program has already started; so you are anxious to get the job done. Could you pour the eggs from one container to the other?

[*Hold the full container as if to pour the eggs into the empty one.*] Your mother would stop that. She would tell you to have the patience to do the job right. Take one egg at a time and put it into the other container. [*Illustrate.*] That is being patient.

Some people think that God is slow because Judgment Day has not come. Jesus told us that He would come back to judge the world. But that was over 1900 years ago, and He hasn't come yet. It seems He might be slow. But Peter says in our Bible reading: "The Lord is not slow about His promise as some count slowness, but is forbearing toward you, not wishing that any should perish, but that all should reach repentance. But the day of the Lord will come like a thief."

God is not slow. He is patient. It takes time to transfer the eggs from one container to the other. They would break if you poured them. The reason why Jesus has not returned to judge us is that He wants to give all people more time to learn about His grace. He does not want to come to judge the world in order to send people to hell. He wants to come to take people to heaven. He wants all people.

Therefore He is patient. He waits for us to learn more about His great love for us. He waits for more people to learn about Him. But that does not mean that He will not come. He is coming. We don't know when, but we know that He is coming as a loving Savior. As you wait for Him, do not think His delay is caused by slowness. Instead remember that it is additional proof of His love for you and all people. Amen.

Security Is Not a Burglar Alarm

The Word

But as to the times and the seasons, brethren, you have no need to have anything written to you. For you yourselves know well that the day of the Lord will come like a thief in the night. 1 Thessalonians 5:1-2 (From the Epistle for the Last Sunday After Trinity)

The World

A large tin can with one end cut out and a light string running through a small hole in the other end (Tie several spoons to the string on the inside of the can to make a burglar alarm.)

If you heard that a burglar was robbing homes in your neighborhood, you might decide that you need a burglar alarm. You could make one like this. [*Show alarm.*] See, these spoons are tied inside the can by this string. You could tie the string across the door of your bedroom with the can hanging from a table or chair. [*Let the can hang over front of lectern.*] If a burglar opened the door, the string would break and the can would fall. That would make a lot of noise. It is a good homemade burglar alarm. Security is having a good burglar alarm. Is it?

Think what would happen if you were asleep some night when [*break the string*] the can fell. The noise would wake you up. But what good would that do you? If your bedroom door is already open, the burglar would already be in your room. This alarm is too late to help you. Security is not a burglar alarm. Security is locked doors so no one can get in unless he has the key to your house. The ones with keys are not thieves but members of the family.

Our Bible reading tells us that Jesus will come sometime when we don't expect Him. St. Paul said, "For you yourselves know well that the day of the Lord will come like a thief in the night." You and I will know when He comes. We don't have to worry about missing Him when He comes. The angels will announce His arrival. But we do not know when He is coming. We cannot wait until He comes to get ready for Him. The angels' announcement that Christ has returned to judge us will be like the burglar alarm in your bedroom. It means He has already arrived. There will be no security in knowing that He has come if we are afraid when He comes. There is no security if we dread His coming.

But you have nothing to be afraid of, nothing to dread. The Christ who is coming comes as a friend. If you had a friend who was coming sometime but you didn't know when, you would not put up a burglar alarm to warn you of His arrival. Instead, you would give him a key so he could come into your house whenever he arrived. We need no alarm to warn us that Christ is coming. When St. Paul says that "the day of the Lord" will come like a thief in the night, it means only that Jesus will come without announcing the exact hour ahead of time. He is coming to give us everything He has promised.

Security is not in knowing that we have an alarm to warn us when Christ is here. Security is in knowing that Christ has the key to our lives. He made that key Himself when He died in our place to forgive our sins. He uses that key to come into our lives each time we hear of His love. We welcome Him now and we will welcome Him on His great Day. Amen.